P9-APW-657

HIGH SCHOOL DROPOUT, GRADUATION, AND COMPLETION RATES

Better Data, Better Measures, Better Decisions

Committee for Improved Measurement of High School Dropout and Completion Rates: Expert Guidance on Next Steps for Research and Policy Workshop

Robert M. Hauser and Judith Anderson Koenig, *Editors*

Center for Education
Division of Behavioral and Social Sciences and Education

NATIONAL RESEARCH COUNCIL *and* NATIONAL ACADEMY OF EDUCATION

THE NATIONAL ACADEMIES PRESS
Washington, D.C.
www.nap.edu

THE NATIONAL ACADEMIES PRESS 500 Fifth Street, N.W. Washington, DC 20001

This study was supported by Award No. B 8143 between the National Academy of Sciences and the Carnegie Corporation of New York. Any opinions, findings, conclusions, or recommendations expressed in this publication are those of the author(s) and do not necessarily reflect the views of the organizations or agencies that provided support for the project.

International Standard Book Number-13:   978-0-309-16307-1
International Standard Book Number-10:   0-309-16307-2

Additional copies of this report are available from the National Academies Press, 500 Fifth Street, N.W., Lockbox 285, Washington, DC 20055; (800) 624-6242 or (202) 334-3313 (in the Washington metropolitan area); Internet, http://www.nap.edu.

Suggested citation: National Research Council and National Academy of Education. (2011). *High School Dropout, Graduation, and Completion Rates: Better Data, Better Measures, Better Decisions*. Committee for Improved Measurement of High School Dropout and Completion Rates: Expert Guidance on Next Steps for Research and Policy Workshop. R.M. Hauser and J.A. Koenig, Editors. Center for Education, Division of Behavioral and Social Sciences and Education. Washington, DC: The National Academies Press.

THE NATIONAL ACADEMIES
Advisers to the Nation on Science, Engineering, and Medicine

The **National Academy of Sciences** is a private, nonprofit, self-perpetuating society of distinguished scholars engaged in scientific and engineering research, dedicated to the furtherance of science and technology and to their use for the general welfare. Upon the authority of the charter granted to it by the Congress in 1863, the Academy has a mandate that requires it to advise the federal government on scientific and technical matters. Dr. Ralph J. Cicerone is president of the National Academy of Sciences.

The **National Academy of Engineering** was established in 1964, under the charter of the National Academy of Sciences, as a parallel organization of outstanding engineers. It is autonomous in its administration and in the selection of its members, sharing with the National Academy of Sciences the responsibility for advising the federal government. The National Academy of Engineering also sponsors engineering programs aimed at meeting national needs, encourages education and research, and recognizes the superior achievements of engineers. Dr. Charles M. Vest is president of the National Academy of Engineering.

The **Institute of Medicine** was established in 1970 by the National Academy of Sciences to secure the services of eminent members of appropriate professions in the examination of policy matters pertaining to the health of the public. The Institute acts under the responsibility given to the National Academy of Sciences by its congressional charter to be an adviser to the federal government and, upon its own initiative, to identify issues of medical care, research, and education. Dr. Harvey V. Fineberg is president of the Institute of Medicine.

The **National Research Council** was organized by the National Academy of Sciences in 1916 to associate the broad community of science and technology with the Academy's purposes of furthering knowledge and advising the federal government. Functioning in accordance with general policies determined by the Academy, the Council has become the principal operating agency of both the National Academy of Sciences and the National Academy of Engineering in providing services to the government, the public, and the scientific and engineering communities. The Council is administered jointly by both Academies and the Institute of Medicine. Dr. Ralph J. Cicerone and Dr. Charles M. Vest are chair and vice chair, respectively, of the National Research Council.

www.national-academies.org

```
NATIONAL
ACADEMY
    of
EDUCATION
```

The **National Academy of Education** advances the highest quality education research and its use in policy formation and practice. Founded in 1965, NAEd consists of U.S. members and foreign associates who are elected on the basis of outstanding scholarship or contributions to education. Since its establishment, NAEd has undertaken commissions and study panels that address pressing issues in education and that typically include both NAEd members and other scholars with an expertise in a particular area of inquiry. In addition, members are deeply engaged in NAEd's professional development fellowship programs focused on the rigorous preparation of the next generation of scholars.

Preface

High school graduation and dropout rates have long been used as a central indicator of education system productivity and effectiveness and of social and economic well-being. Today, interest in the accuracy and usefulness of these statistics is particularly acute because of changing demographics, new legislative mandates, and heightened political pressures to reduce the numbers and rates of dropouts. Despite this strong need for sound and reliable measures of high school dropout and completion rates, there has been widespread disagreement among researchers, statisticians, and policy analysts about the "true" rates, how they are best measured, and what trends are evident over time. At a time when policy makers are vitally interested in tracking the incidence of dropping out of school, they are faced with choosing among substantially discrepant estimates that would lead them to different conclusions regarding both the size of the dropout problem and how it has changed in recent years.

In 2008 the National Research Council (NRC) and the National Academy of Education decided to jointly undertake a project focused on improving understanding of these rates and specifically (1) to explore the strengths, weaknesses, and accuracy of available rates; (2) to gather information on the state of the art with respect to constructing longitudinal student accounting systems for measuring dropout and completion rates; (3) to identify the kinds of analyses that are needed in order to understand changes in the rates; and (4) to consider ways that information on dropout and completion rates can used to improve practice at the local level and public policies at the state and national levels. The project was funded by the Carnegie Corporation. A steering committee was formed to convene a workshop addressing these topics and to make recommendations about best practices in calculating and reporting dropout and completion rates. The committee members were chosen for their expertise in education research, policy, and administration; education statistics and data systems; school organization; school-leaving processes; and minority education.

The Workshop on Improved Measurement of High School Dropout and Completion Rates: Expert Guidance on Next Steps for Research and Policy was held on October 23 and 24, 2008, in Washington, DC. The workshop agenda and a list of participants are in Appendix A. Biographical sketches of committee members and staff appear in Appendix B. The background papers and workshop transcript are posted on the NRC website at http://www7. nationalacademies.org/bota/High_School_Dropouts_Workshop_Agenda.html.

Many people contributed to the success of this project. The committee first expresses its appreciation to the members of the Research Advisory Committee of the National Academy of Education, chaired by Alan Schoenfeld, University of California, Berkeley. I am grateful to my colleagues on that committee for their leadership and support in bringing this project to fruition, including: Richard Atkinson, University of California; James Banks, University of Washington; Margaret Eisenhart, University of Colorado, Boulder; Michael Feuer, National Research Council; Ellen Lagemann, Bard College; Michael McPherson, Spencer Foundation; Lauren Resnick, University of Pittsburgh; Lorrie Shepard, University of Colorado, Boulder; and Marshall Smith, William and Flora Hewlett Foundation. We also gratefully acknowledge the contributions of Gregory White, executive director, and Andrea Solarz, director of research initiatives, both with the National Academy of Education; both offered many helpful suggestions throughout the course of this project.

On behalf of the committee, we also acknowledge the scholars who wrote papers and made presentations at the workshop, which provided the intellectual foundations for this report: Robert Balfanz, Johns Hopkins University; Wesley Bruce, Indiana Department of Education; Robert Curtin, Massachusetts Department of Education; Noelle Ellerson, American Association of School Administrators; Delegate Ana Sol Gutiérrez, Maryland State Legislature; Jeanine Hildreth, Baltimore City Schools; Dan Losen, Civil Rights Project; Deborah Newby, U.S. Department of Education; Aaron Pallas, Teachers College, Columbia University; Mel Riddile, National Association of Secondary School Principals; Richard Rothstein, Economics Policy Institute; Bill Smith, Sioux Falls School District, South Dakota; Nancy Smith, Data Quality Campaign; Chris Swanson, Editorial Projects in Education; Robin Taylor, Delaware Department of Education; and David Wakelyn, National Governors Association.

The committee also thanks the NRC staff of the Board on Testing and Assessment who worked on this project: Kelly Duncan, senior project assistant, for her expert skills in organizing the workshop and two committee meetings; Rose Neugroschel, research assistant, for her careful attention to detail in finalizing this manuscript; and director Stuart Elliott, for his contributions in formulating the workshop design and making it a reality. We especially thank Judy Koenig for her intellectual and organizational skills as the study director. And we thank Patricia Morison, associate executive director of the Division of Behavioral and Social Sciences and Education for her support and guidance at key stages in this project.

Finally, as chair of the committee, I thank the committee members for their dedication and outstanding contributions to this project. They actively assisted in all stages of this project, including planning the workshop and identifying presenters, preparing papers and leading workshop discussions, and writing and rewriting multiple versions of this report. They gave generously of their time to ensure that the final product accurately represents the workshop discussions, is understandable to a variety of audiences, and fully portrays the complex issues associated with calculating dropout and completion rates. We particularly acknowledge Elaine Allensworth's contribution to Chapter 3, Rob Warren's contribution to Chapter 4, Lavan Dukes' contribution to Chapter 6, and Russ Rumberger's contribution to Chapter 7.

This report has been reviewed in draft form by individuals chosen for their diverse perspectives and technical expertise, in accordance with procedures approved by the NRC's Report Review Committee. The purpose of this independent review is to provide candid and critical comments that will assist the institution in making its published report as sound as possible and to ensure that the report meets institutional standards for objectivity, evidence, and responsiveness to the study charge. The review comments and draft manuscript remain confidential to protect the integrity of the deliberative process. We thank the following individuals for their review of this report: Wes Bruce, Department of Education, State of Indiana; Duncan Chaplin, Human Services Research Division, Mathematica Policy Research, Inc.; Alan F. Karr, Director's Office, National Institute of Statistical Sciences; Ruth Lopez Turley, Department of Sociology, University of Wisconsin, Madison; Samuel R. Lucas, Department of Sociology, University of California, Berkeley; Richard J. Murnane, Graduate School of Education, Harvard University; Stephen W. Raudenbush, Department of Sociology, University of Chicago; and Julian Vasquez Heilig, University Council for Educational Administration, Department of Education Administration, University of Texas, Austin.

Although the reviewers listed above have provided many constructive comments and suggestions, they were not asked to endorse the conclusions or recommendations nor did they see the final draft of the report before its release. The review of this report was overseen by Lorraine McDonnell, University of California, Santa Barbara, and Lawrence D. Brown, Department of Statistics,

Wharton School, University of Pennsylvania. Appointed by the NRC, they were responsible for making certain that an independent examination of this report was carried out in accordance with institutional procedures and that all review comments were carefully considered. Responsibility for the final content of this report rests entirely with the authoring committee and the institution.

Robert M. Hauser, *Chair*
Committee for Improved Measurement of
High School Dropout and Completion
Rates: Expert Guidance on Next Steps for
Research and Policy Workshop

Contents

Summary

High school graduation and dropout rates have long been used as indicators of educational system productivity and effectiveness and of social and economic well-being.

While determining these rates may seem like a straightforward task, their calculation is in fact quite complicated. How does one count a student who leaves a regular high school but later obtains a General Educational Development (GED) credential? How does one count a student who spends most of his/her high school years at one school and then transfers to another? If the student graduates, which school should receive credit? If the student drops out, which school should take responsibility?

The Committee on Improved Measurement of High School Dropout and Completion Rates was asked to address these issues and to examine (1) the strengths, limitations, accuracy, and utility of the available dropout and completion measures; (2) the state of the art with respect to longitudinal data systems; and (3) ways that dropout and completion rates can be used to improve policy and practice.

THE RATES AND HOW THEY ARE CALCULATED

In their simplest sense, graduation rates reflect the percentage of students who earned a regular high school diploma, and dropout rates reflect the percentage of students who did not. However, the requirements for earning a regular diploma vary widely among states and districts, and there are multiple means of completing school besides earning a regular diploma after attending

1

high school for four years. Students may obtain a GED, a certificate of attendance, or another alternative type of diploma. They may take longer than the typical 4 years before completing high school and may transfer across schools or districts before graduating or dropping out. There are a variety of strategies for accounting for these factors in calculating dropout, completion, and graduation rates; different strategies will affect the appropriateness of the rate for a given purpose. Thus, decisions about how to handle these factors should be consistent with the purpose for calculating the rate.

For example, if the purpose is to describe the level of education of the population, what matters is people's eventual level of education, not what kind of diploma they received or how long it took them to earn it. But if the purpose is to evaluate a school's effectiveness in graduating students in 4 years, those factors are of critical importance. All methods for calculating the rates require decisions about who to include in the numerator and denominator of the rate and how to handle certain groups of students, such as those who receive a GED or who take longer than four years to graduate.

We recommend that analysts and users keep their purpose in mind when selecting from among the various kinds of rates and choose the indicator best suited to that purpose (Recommendation 4-1[1]). To help users draw sound conclusions, analysts should document the limitations of the rate and the decisions that went into calculating it (Recommendations 3-1 and 3-2). When the limitations are made explicit, alternative rates can be calculated to verify any conclusions drawn from the statistic (Recommendations 3-3 and 3-4).

The most accurate rates are those based on longitudinal data that track students over the course of their schooling, and we recommend that dropout and completion rates be based on individual student-level data whenever possible. This will allow for the greatest flexibility and transparency with respect to how analysts handle methodological issues that arise in defining the numerator and denominator of the rates (Recommendation 4-2).

BUILDING DATA SYSTEMS

Calculating rates based on individual data requires that states have a system for tracking students over time. At a minimum, such a system needs unique student identifiers as well as complete information on students' enrollment status throughout high school. However, a more comprehensive system would incorporate data elements that allow school systems to monitor students' progress, identify students at risk of dropping out, and evaluate the effectiveness of programs to reduce dropping out. To perform these functions, data systems require detailed longitudinal data (Recommendation 6-1).

---

[1]Recommendation 4-1 is the first recommendation in Chapter 4. Other recommendations are numbered accordingly.

Producing accurate rates requires that states and districts adopt procedures to ensure the quality of their data; we, therefore, recommend that all states and districts maintain written documentation of their processes, procedures, and results. The documentation should be updated annually and should include a process for adding elements or making changes to the system (Recommendation 6-2).

Because the quality of the data begins at the point when data are collected and entered into the system, it is important that training be provided for those who carry out these tasks. We recommend that all states and districts implement a system of extensive and on-going staff training that addresses procedures for collection, storage, analysis, and use of the data (Recommendation 6-3) and conduct regular audits to verify data quality (Recommendation 6-4).

HOW DATA SYSTEMS CAN IMPROVE POLICY AND PRACTICE

Improving graduation rates in this country requires more than simply reporting accurate rates. To truly improve outcomes for students, data systems need to incorporate information that enables early identification of at-risk students. Research suggests a number of factors associated with dropping out: frequent absences, failing grades in reading or math, poor behavior, being over age for grade, having a low grade 9 grade-point average (GPA), failing grade 9, or having a record of frequent transfers. These findings suggest that states and districts should build data systems that incorporate documented early indicators of the risk of dropping out. At the same time, they should also conduct their own studies to determine the factors associated with dropping out from their school systems. Once determined, measures of these factors should be incorporated into the data system so at-risk students can be identified in time to intervene (Recommendation 5-1).

Finally, the federal government should play an active role in this area by collecting data on these early indicators. These indicators should be collected by grade level and should include variables such as the number of students missing a month or more of school, average number of days absent, average number of course failures, number of students failing one course or more, mean GPA, and indicators of behavior problems. Collecting these data would allow for indications of progress toward graduation at the national level and enable comparative studies on early indicators of dropout across states and localities (Recommendation 7-4).

As educational accountability focuses increasingly on the successful completion of high school, appropriate, relevant, and understandable measures of high school dropout and completion are becoming more important as indicators of the functioning of schools and of students' preparation for college and work. The findings and recommendations of this report are provided to guide the creation of such indicators at the local, state, and national levels.

1

Introduction

High school graduation and dropout rates have long been used as a central indicator of education system productivity and effectiveness and of social and economic well-being. Today, interest in the accuracy and usefulness of these statistics is particularly acute owing to a confluence of circumstances, including changing demographics, new legislative mandates, and heightened political pressures to reduce the incidence of dropping out. The population of American school-age children is shifting from native whites toward minorities and immigrants, populations that have a higher risk of dropping out; the new regime of educational accountability, especially the movement toward testing for promotion and graduation, has raised fears of a secondary effect on school dropout rates. In other words, students who are unable to pass these assessments may simply leave school before graduating. In addition, the No Child Left Behind (NCLB) Act of 2002 specifically requires an indicator of educational progress other than test scores at the high school level. Timely high school graduation appears to be the indicator of choice.

HIGH SCHOOL DROPOUT AND GRADUATION RATES

Despite the strong need for sound and reliable measures of high school dropout and completion, there has been widespread disagreement among researchers, statisticians, and policy analysts about the "true" rates, how they are best measured, and what trends are evident over time. Recently, a number of analysts have argued that the growing importance of alternative high school credentials, combined with various technical problems and political pressures, has led to serious overreporting of "official" high school graduation rates. Their analyses produce national graduation rates of about 70 percent overall and 50 percent for minorities, numbers that are lower than those reported on the basis of official government sources (e.g., *Education Week*, 2009; Greene and Winters, 2002; Warren, 2004). Some researchers also contend that this problem of overreporting the graduation rate has been getting worse over time (Heckman and LaFontaine, 2008, 2010). Others (e.g., Mishel and Roy, 2006) counter that these analyses are incorrect and that the graduation rate, while still unacceptably low, has been accurately reported in national government surveys and has not changed appreciably over the past 20 years. Similar discrepancies, depending on data sources and the analyses conducted, exist in dropout and graduation estimates at state and local levels. At a time when policy makers are vitally interested in tracking the incidence of dropping out of school, they are faced with choosing among substantially discrepant estimates that would lead them to different conclusions regarding both the size of the dropout problem and how it has changed in recent years.

DATA SOURCES USED FOR ESTIMATES

Estimates of these rates are derived from a variety of sources using a variety of procedures. National estimates are derived from both cross-sectional and longitudinal sample surveys. The Current Population Survey (CPS) conducted by the U.S. Census Bureau is a nationally representative cross-sectional household survey that asks detailed questions about educational enrollment and experiences in October of each year. The National Center for Education Statistics (NCES) and the Bureau of Labor Statistics periodically conduct longitudinal surveys that track representative samples of youth through the usual high school years and beyond.

School administrative records on enrollments, dropouts, and diplomas have typically been used by states and school districts for reporting these rates. These data are reported annually to NCES as part of the Common Core of Data (CCD) collection of information on public schools in the country and have also been used to generate national, state, and district estimates of dropout and completion rates. Many states and school districts now have longitudinal unit-record administrative data systems that allow them to track the progress of individual students over time. However, decisions about ways to handle specific groups of students (e.g., students who transfer or who leave school but obtain a high school equivalency credential, like the General Educational Development [GED]) can affect the statistics that are calculated, even when the same formulas are used to calculate the rates.

Each data source brings with it a unique set of issues that can substantially affect the quality and usefulness of dropout rate statistics. Rates derived from sample-based surveys (both cross-sectional and longitudinal) have been criticized because they rely on respondent self-reports (Heckman and LaFontaine, 2008, 2010), and some have questioned the degree to which longitudinal data accurately track disadvantaged populations (see National Research Council, 2010). Rates estimated from aggregated counts in administrative data systems have been questioned when adjustments are not made to control for repeating ninth graders or to account for transfer students (Warren, 2005). The ways that states and local school districts classify students as dropouts, graduates, or completers can significantly affect the rates that are calculated.

Whatever the data source, there are also major questions in defining both an appropriate numerator and a denominator in calculating these rates. For example, should it include private school enrollees? Recent émigrés enrolled in U.S. schools but who spent most of their education outside the U.S. education system? GED recipients? Special education students? "On-time" graduates only? Obviously, these choices should be driven by the policy questions being addressed as well as the availability of the desired data. However, until recently, no standard conventions for data inclusion or exclusion have been widely accepted in the education research and policy community. Efforts by the National Governors Association represent some progress toward standardizing methods for estimating graduation rates (National Governors Association Task Force on State High School Graduation Data, 2005). Nevertheless, there remains a lack of understanding about which calculation methods and which data are most appropriate for different policy questions, and often the best data sources may not be available for the calculations.

COMMITTEE CHARGE

The Committee for Improved Measurement of High School Dropout and Completion Rates was formed to convene a workshop and to make recommendations about these issues. Specifically, the steering committee was asked to address the following questions:

1. What are the available measures of dropout and completion rates, how are they determined, and what are their strengths and limitations?
2. To what extent do current and proposed measures attain the necessary levels of accuracy, given the types of policy decision that they inform?
3. What is the state of the art with respect to constructing longitudinal student accounting systems for measuring dropout and completion rates? What is the feasibility and desirability of moving to such systems? What are some of the issues that need to be considered when designing these data systems?
4. In what ways can the analysis of data from current and proposed systems for measuring dropout and completion rates be used to help understand changes in the rates?

5.   How can this information be used to improve practice at the local level and improve public policies at the state and national levels?

In response to the charge, the committee organized a workshop designed to explore the strengths and weaknesses of various kinds of rates, the policy decisions based on them, and the kinds of data required to inform those policy decisions. The committee began this task by conducting a review of the literature. The topic addressed by this project—dropping out of high school—is one that has been studied in great depth, and the literature base is quite expansive. A review of the entire literature base was beyond the scope and resources of this study. The committee therefore focused its review on research explicitly related to its charge: studies on the calculation of dropout and completion rates, the information needed to calculate them, and the policy uses of these rates. The committee also conducted a limited review of research on the relationships between education attainment and social and economic outcomes. This review was designed to provide context for the work and to document the value of reporting dropout and completion rates, but it was not intended to be an exhaustive review of the literature on this topic. Based on this review, the committee identified the researchers who have been actively pursuing this line of study and invited a subset of them to participate in the workshop. The committee also recruited a set of policy makers, practitioners, and stakeholders to discuss these issues during the workshop.

The workshop was held on October 23 and 24, 2008, and consisted of four panels of speakers. The first panel focused on policy uses of these rates, and panelists represented different administrative levels of the education system in this country (i.e., national, state, district, and school). The second panel made presentations about methods for calculating the rates, including discussion of the decisions required and the strengths and weaknesses of the methods. The third panel focused on development of longitudinal databases and included representatives from state and local school districts, who talked about their work to develop these systems. The final panel addressed the issue of how these data systems can be used to improve policy and practice. This panel focused specifically on early indicators of students at risk of dropping out and how this research could be used to better inform policy and practice. The workshop agenda appears in Appendix A, along with a list of workshop participants and guests. The papers and presentations from this workshop, the research that the presenters referenced, and the information that the committee gathered as part of its own literature review served as the basis for this report and the committee's recommendations.

IMPORTANT TERMS

Throughout this report, we use several terms that warrant clarification. We use the term "graduate" to refer to a student who earns a regular high school diploma and "graduation rate" as an indicator of the percentage of students in a given population who earned a regular high school diploma. We note, however, that the definition of "regular diploma" may vary as well as the time allowed to complete it. We use the term "completer" as the all-encompassing term to refer to a student who finished high school via one of multiple ways, such as by earning a regular high school diploma, a GED, or another type of certificate (a certificate of attendance, certificate of completion, etc.). Likewise, "completion rate" indicates the percentage of students in a given population who finished high school in any of these ways. We use the term "dropout" to refer to a student who did not complete high school and "dropout rate" as an indicator of the percentage of students in a given population who did not complete high school. Dropouts may include those who earn a GED or an alternative credential (depending on the specific indicator or the purpose of the indicator), but the group does not include students still enrolled in school after they were expected to complete. There are a number of policy definitions of these terms that further specify them (e.g., NCLB specifies that the graduation rate should include only on-time diploma earners, and it classifies GED recipients with dropouts). Unless otherwise specified in the report, we use the terms in their most general sense.

There are four general categories of dropout/completion indicators, which are defined below.

1. *Individual cohort rate:* a rate derived from longitudinal data on a population of individuals who share a common characteristic at one point in time, such as entering high school. The rate is based on tracking the students over the 4 years of high school or more to determine which of them graduated and which of them dropped out.
2. *Aggregate cohort rate:* a rate designed to approximate an individual cohort rate when longitudinal data are not available by using aggregate counts of students (e.g., number of ninth graders in a given year, number of graduates in a given year). For instance, an aggregate cohort rate might compare the number of students who graduate in one year with the number of students who entered high school 4 years earlier.
3. *Status rate:* a rate that represents the fraction of a population that falls into a certain category at a given point of time (e.g., the percentage of the total U.S. population that does not have a high school diploma).
4. *Event rate:* a rate that is the fraction of a population that experiences a particular event over a given time interval. For instance, the event dropout rate indicates the percentage of students who exit school during a specific academic year without having earned a diploma.

ORGANIZATION OF THE REPORT

This report summarizes the proceedings from the workshop. Following this introduction, Chapter 2 draws on the presentations from the first panel and explains why these rates are important and how they are used for policy purposes. Based on information presented during the second panel discussion, Chapter 3 discusses the decisions that must be made in calculating these rates, and Chapter 4 explores the different types of rates and their uses. An important use of dropout and completion rates is to identify which students are likely to drop out and when they are most at risk in order to implement programs and/or interventions aimed at keeping students in school. Chapter 5 draws from several of the workshop presentations and discusses the research on early indicators of dropping out as well as on building data systems that incorporate these indicators to enable early identification of at-risk students. Chapter 6 continues the discussion of database development and summarizes the presentations made by state and district representatives participating in the third panel. Chapter 7 lays out ways the data systems can be used to improve policy and practice. The committee's conclusions and recommendations are presented at the end of each chapter and are summarized in Chapter 8. The workshop agenda appears in Appendix A, along with a list of workshop participants and guests. Biographical sketches of committee members and staff appear in Appendix B.

2

Dropout Rates, Graduation Rates, and Public Policy

There is widespread agreement that failure to earn a high school diploma is a serious problem in this country. A considerable body of research has documented the individual and societal costs associated with dropping out and demonstrates the many hardships that dropouts face. Most people agree that the nation's dropout rate is too high and the graduation rate is unacceptably low. However, determining the full extent of the problem has been difficult due to disagreements about how to calculate the rates: it is difficult to remediate a problem when its exact nature is still in dispute. Numerous policy measures have been targeted at improving the educational attainment of young people in this country, but it is hard to evaluate their effectiveness without accurate, consistent estimates of graduation and dropout rates.

In this chapter, we explore a series of issues intended to provide context for the report. The chapter is separated into three sections. It begins with a brief summary of the literature on the social and economic outcomes experienced by individuals who fail to earn a high school diploma in order to document why it is important to have accurate and consistent estimates of the rates that provide a clear sense of the problem. In the second section, we discuss some of the discrepancies in the rates that have been reported, beginning with a description of the data sources used to produce the rates and the differences among them that contribute to these discrepancies. The chapter concludes with a discussion of the policy attention the rates have received, with a focus on their use in the accountability system established by the No Child Left Behind (NCLB) Act of 2001. We close the chapter with our recommendation for the ways that dropout and completion rates should be incorporated into accountability policy.

At the Workshop on Improved Measurement of High School Dropout and Completion Rates: Expert Guidance on Next Steps for Research and Policy, a series of presentations discussed why it is important to report dropout and graduation rates and how they are used for public policy. These presentations serve as the basis for the information in this chapter, particularly papers by Dan Losen, with the Civil Rights Project (Losen, 2008), and Richard Rothstein, with the Economic Policy Institute (Rothstein, 2008). We supplemented these presentations with our own review of the relevant literature, as further explained in each section of this chapter.

SOCIAL AND ECONOMIC OUTCOMES ASSOCIATED WITH EDUCATIONAL ATTAINMENT

There is a wide body of research on the social and economic outcomes associated with educational attainment. A review of these studies reveals that individuals who fail to earn a high school diploma are clearly disadvantaged in many aspects of life—from the jobs they obtain and the wages they earn to their sense of physical and emotional well-being. Society is also disadvantaged when students drop out, since studies show that dropouts are less likely than graduates to contribute to the social and economic well-being of the country.

For the most part, this literature consists of studies that are descriptive in nature, documenting the differences in outcomes for individuals with and without a high school diploma. It is important to note that most of them do not support inferences about the factors that *cause* individuals who dropout to experience economic and social hardships. Attributing cause in this line of research is difficult for several reasons. One complexity is that the factors that cause students to drop out are also factors that cause people to not do well in other aspects of life. That is, students who drop out often have low achievement and low motivation, factors that contribute to poor performance in school and poor functioning in society (Rumberger, forthcoming). These and other personal attributes may be the underlying cause of the poor social and economic outcomes experienced by this group; dropping out may be a symptom of the problem rather than the cause.

Another complexity stems from the fact that it is difficult to design the kinds of studies that allow one to attribute cause, such as by conducting experiments that make use of random assignment. Clearly, individuals cannot be randomly assigned to be dropouts or graduates. Studies that employ advanced techniques, such as model fitting or regression discontinuity analyses, also can support causal inference; however, only a few studies have used these techniques.[1]

---

[1]Studies that are designed in a way to support causal inferences fall into two general categories. The first consists of studies that permit causal inferences about the benefits of acquiring a particu-

Nevertheless, a number of negative outcomes associated with dropping out are consistently reported in this body of research. The fact that these findings are corroborated by multiple independent studies permits a certain degree of confidence in the conclusions that can be drawn, even though they are based primarily on descriptive rather than experimental studies.[2] Below we discuss these findings, specifically comparing social and economic outcomes for graduates, dropouts, and individuals who receive a General Educational Development (GED) credential. This review is not intended to be an exhaustive examination of the literature but simply an overview designed to give the reader a general sense of the differences in outcomes for individuals with and without high school diplomas.

OUTCOMES FOR GRADUATES AND DROPOUTS

Earning a high school diploma is one of the most important factors associated with social and economic success in America. A high school diploma signifies that the bearer has both the cognitive and noncognitive attributes important for success in adulthood. It is usually a minimum requirement for engaging in further training and serves as the gatekeeper for higher education and higher paying jobs. Research shows that high school graduates fare better than dropouts in many aspects of life (Belfield and Levin, 2007). Dropouts are more likely to become teenage parents and have nonmarital births (Manlove, 1998; McLanahan, 2009). They are less likely to vote or engage in civic activities (Bartels, 2008; Uslaner and Brown, 2005). They have poorer prospects for intergenerational mobility (McLanahan, 2009).

Graduates and dropouts differ markedly in their labor market outcomes, although, as noted above, it cannot always be inferred that these differences are caused by the education credential. Graduates are more likely to be employed than dropouts, and their wages are higher. Government data show that 58.9 percent of students who dropped out of school in the 2006-07 school year were not working (unemployed or not in the labor force) the following October (http://nces.ed.gov/programs/digest/d08/tables/dt08_389.asp). Among all 16- to 24-year-olds in October 2007, the unemployment rate for dropouts was 17.3

---

lar credential. Some examples include the following. Oreopoulos (2007) and Oreopoulous and Salvanes (2009) studied the impact of credentials on a variety of types of outcomes. Tyler, Murnane, and Willett (2000) and Tyler (2003) studied labor market outcomes. Lochner and Moretti (2004) and Moretti (2007) studied involvement in criminal activities. Lleras-Muney (2005) and Cutler and Lleras-Muney (2006) studied health outcomes. A second category consists of studies that permit causal inferences about the effects of particular programs designed to achieve objectives, such as to increase the high school graduation rate. Examples are U.S. Department of Education (2008a, 2008b) and Levin and Belfield (2007).

[2]For further discussion about making causal inferences, see National Research Council (2002, pp. 110-117).

percent, compared with 11.6 percent for high school graduates and 5.5 percent for 4-year college graduates (http://nces.ed.gov/programs/digest/d08/tables/dt08_382.asp). Even if they find a job, dropouts earn substantially less than high school graduates. In 2007, the median annual earnings of high school dropouts were 29 percent less for men and 33 percent less for women, compared with the earnings of high school graduates (http://nces.ed.gov/programs/digest/d08/tables/dt08_384.asp). The U.S. Census Bureau estimates that over their working lives, dropouts will earn about $200,000 less than high school graduates (Day and Newburger, 2002, Figure 3).

High school graduates also tend to live a longer and healthier life than dropouts. Research shows that, on average, a high school graduate lives 6 to 9 years longer than a dropout (Wong et al., 2002) and that there appears to be a positive relationship between educational attainment and health status (Currie, 2009; Cutler and Lleras-Muney, 2006; Pleis and Lucas, 2009; Ross and Wu, 1995). A number of factors may contribute to this. For one, individuals with low educational attainment may have difficulty understanding doctor's instructions and health-related literature, and consequently may be more likely to make poor health decisions. In addition, smoking is more prevalent among individuals with lower income and education levels. According to a survey conducted by the National Institutes of Health (NIH) in 2007, 28.1 percent of adults who are poor and 25.4 percent of adults who are near poor are smokers, compared with 17.7 percent of individuals who are not poor (Pleis and Lucas, 2009, Table 25). The researchers also found that adults with at least a bachelor's degree were less likely to be current or former smokers than those with less education.

Dropouts are also less likely than high school graduates to report that they exercise regularly, and they are more likely to be obese. In a recent survey, Pleis and Lucas (2009, p. 12) found that 84 percent of adults with less than a high school diploma reported that they "never engage in periods of vigorous leisure-time physical activity as compared with 46 percent of adults with a bachelor's degree or higher." Roughly 29 percent of high school dropouts are considered to be obese, compared with 20 percent of college graduates (Centers for Disease Control and Prevention, 2008). Cardiovascular disease, respiratory disease, and diabetes are all higher among less educated people (Muennig, 2005; Pleis and Lucas, 2009).

There is also evidence of a relationship between emotional well-being and educational attainment. Pleis and Lucas (2009) report that feelings of sadness, hopelessness, and worthlessness are most prevalent among adults with less education than a high school diploma.

Studies also show that educational attainment appears to be related to participation in criminal behavior, in that those with higher levels of education are less likely to commit crimes, get arrested, or become incarcerated (Farrington, 2003; Levin et al., 2007). The relationship between dropout status and incarceration appears to be quite strong: although dropouts constitute less than 20 percent of the overall population, they make up 41 percent of the incarcerated population (Harlow, 2003, reporting data for 1997). In contrast, although those with a high school diploma make up roughly 33 percent of the population, they make up only 23 percent of the incarcerated population. There is also a striking relationship between race, education, and incarceration. For example, Western and Wildeman (2009) found that the risk of imprisonment was three to four times higher for white and black male dropouts compared with high school graduates, with the risk of imprisonment for black dropouts at 69 percent. In addition, dropouts are about three and a half times more likely than high school graduates to be arrested (Coalition for Juvenile Justice, 2001). These data underscore the point that although many dropouts do not participate in criminal behaviors, individuals who are arrested or are incarcerated are more likely to be dropouts than to have earned a diploma.

OUTCOMES FOR GENERAL EDUCATIONAL DEVELOPMENT RECIPIENTS

Students who leave school but earn a GED credential generally do not do as well as those who earn a high school diploma. Some studies find that dropouts who earn a GED credential generally have a higher income than dropouts who do not (Murnane, Willett, and Tyler, 2002; Tyler, 2003; Tyler, Murnane, and Willegg, 2003), and there may be more of a payoff for dropouts who left school with weak skills than those who left with higher skills (Murnane et al., 2002; Tyler, 2003). GED recipients do not realize the social and economic benefits that come with a high school diploma, however (Cameron and Heckman, 1993; Heckman and LaFontaine, 2008; Heckman, Humphries, and Mader, 2010). GED recipients make less money than high school graduates (Heckman and Rubenstein, 2001).

The reasons for these differences between graduates and GED recipients are not fully understood (Rothstein, 2008), although some speculate that there are a number of nonacademic attributes—such as motivation, time management, persistence, interpersonal skills, having an orientation toward long-term planning—that contribute to an individual's ability to stay in high school and earn a diploma. These attributes are likely to be related to subsequent performance in college and on the job (Heckman, Humphries, and Mader, 2010; Heckman and Rubinstein, 2001). For instance, Laurence (2008) reports that GED recipients and dropouts have similar attrition rates from the military. Also, Heckman and LaFontaine (2008, forthcoming) report that degree attainment rates are similar for GED recipients and dropouts who pursue postsecondary schooling.

DETERMINING THE EXTENT OF THE DROPOUT PROBLEM

Identification of the extent of the dropout problem is the first step in addressing it and working toward remedies to keep students in school. Any attempt at remediation requires accurate, consistent estimates of these rates. However, the data and methods for calculating the rates differ, and there are considerable differences of opinion about the appropriate procedures (e.g., Greene and Winters, 2002; Heckman and LaFontaine, 2008, 2010; Mishel and Roy, 2006). The resulting rates can differ dramatically and portray different pictures of educational attainment in this country. Below we briefly describe several key data sources, highlight some of the challenges associated with calculating the rates, and discuss the discrepancies in rates that have been reported. Chapters 3 and 4 discuss these issues in more depth.

Data Sources

One source for dropout and graduation rates is nationally collected data. For more than 50 years, information about educational attainment has been available through the Current Population Survey (CPS), conducted by the U.S. Census Bureau. The CPS is a monthly household survey established to provide a direct measurement of monthly unemployment. The CPS includes a series of questions on school enrollment, college attendance, and high school graduation that can be used to calculate an overall dropout rate for the country. One commonly used dropout rate based on these data is the percentage of 16- to 24-year-olds who are not enrolled in school and who have not earned high school credentials. These data cannot be reliably disaggregated below the regional level on an annual basis, however, and there is no way to connect the rates to the schools that the respondents attended. For many years, the CPS was the primary source for calculating dropout rates.

Since the late 1960s, data have also been collected through the State Non-fiscal Survey from the Common Core of Data (CCD), administered by the U.S. Department of Education's National Center for Education Statistics (NCES). The CCD collects data from all public elementary and secondary schools and school districts in the country. The CCD was designed to "provide basic information and descriptive statistics on public elementary and secondary schools and schooling" (Thurgood et al., 2003, p. 19). CCD data are obtained primarily from administrative records in state education agencies. The information collected by the CCD allows estimation of high school completion and dropout rates and can be calculated at the state and local levels. Because they are based on aggregate data, rather than individual student records, however, the rates can become distorted, because student mobility and grade retention cannot be taken into consideration in calculating the rates.

States also publish their own rates based on data they collect themselves, using a variety of different measures and procedures, some of which have the potential to produce upward or downward biases in the rates. Until recently, there were few efforts to understand the differences in these measures or to bring uniformity to the procedures. For instance, in the past, some states reported a graduation rate based on dividing the aggregate number of graduates at the end of the year by the aggregate number of students who started the year in the senior class. This approach misses the majority of dropouts who leave school before grade 12 and can result in an overestimate of the graduation rate. Others have divided the aggregate number of graduates by the aggregate number of students enrolled in grade 9 four years earlier, an approach that may inflate the size of the cohort because of students repeating grade 9. Thus, this approach can produce an underestimate of the graduation rate.

Some states have longitudinal unit-record data systems, are able to track individual students as they move from school to school, and know whether they drop out or continue on to earn a diploma. Yet decisions about how to treat special categories of students can affect the rates. Classifying students who earn a GED credential or special education students who earn a certificate of attendance as graduates exaggerates the success of states in ensuring that students have successfully completed high school coursework and produces overestimates of graduation rates. Removing students from the cohort when they fail the state exit exam or are expelled can also inflate graduation rates. States also have different approaches for dealing with the time it takes a student to complete high school. Some calculate a 4-year rate, and some make no distinction between students who graduate in four years and students who take longer. Some of these problems may result because of inadequate record-keeping systems; others are the result of deliberate efforts to keep official dropout rates low and graduation rates high.

Discrepancies in the Reported Rates

For years, the most frequently reported rate was the CPS national dropout rate. This rate portrayed a rather positive picture about educational attainment in this country, suggesting that the incidence of dropping out was steadily diminishing, from about 15 percent in 1965 to less than 9 percent in 2000 (Cataldi, Laird, and KewalRamani, 2009:Table 7). Based on these reported rates, one might expect a high school completion rate of about 90 percent. However, as data and methods were developed to calculate national, state, and regional completion rates from the CCD, a contrasting picture became apparent. National completion rates based on the CCD appeared to be much lower than the expected 90 percent, showing that high school graduation rates were stable or declining—not increasing—from about 78 percent in 1975 to about 72 percent in 2002 (cited in Warren and Halpern-Manners, 2007).

The discrepancies between the CPS-based and CCD-based rates, as well as the negative findings from the CCD-based estimates, have triggered considerable public attention to measuring the true extent of noncompletion of high school in this country (see, e.g., the cover story in *Time*, April 17, 2006, by Thornburgh). One report that garnered significant public attention was published by Greene (2001, revised in 2002) using CCD data, which found a national graduation rate of only 71 percent for the class of 1998 and much lower rates for minority youths at 56 percent for African American students and 54 percent for Latino students. These estimates were disputed by Mishel and Roy (2006), who, using CPS data, reported a higher overall graduation rate of 82 percent and graduation rates for African Americans and Hispanics of approximately 74 percent.

Greene also reported graduation rates for each state, revealing alarmingly low rates for some states. According to his analyses, Georgia had the lowest overall graduation rate (54 percent), with rates for minorities at 44 percent for African Americans and 32 percent for Latinos. The District of Columbia, Florida, and Nevada followed closely behind with graduation rates below 60 percent. Some of Greene's rates differed markedly from those reported by the state itself. These discrepancies were highlighted in an analysis by the Education Trust (2003), which compared Greene's estimates to states' self-reported rates. In nearly half of the states (n = 24), the self-reported rate was 10 percentage points or more above Greene's estimate. The largest discrepancy was for North Carolina, with a difference of 29 percentage points between the state self-reported rate (92 percent) and Greene's estimate (63 percent).

These low rates and the discrepancies among the estimates have prompted a number of researchers to investigate the sources of the differences (e.g., Heckman and LaFontaine, 2010; Miao and Haney, 2004; Swanson, 2004; Swanson and Chaplin, 2003; Warren and Halpern-Manners, 2007). Differences in the CPS-based and CCD-based rates appear to be attributable to data collection methods (the CPS is a self-reported, sample-based survey; the CCD is a census of school administrative data); how GED recipients are treated (i.e., considered as graduates or not); whether the rate is for dropouts, completers, or graduates; whether rates include public and private school students; and the type of rate calculated (e.g., status, event, cohort). States' rules for classifying students as graduates, completers, and dropouts appear to account for discrepancies in state self-reported rates. These differences are further discussed in Chapters 3 and 4.

GRADUATION RATES AND NCLB

Reports by Greene and others of such low graduation rates have brought renewed attention to the issue, both in the form of advocacy by groups who have worked to increase awareness of the problem and in the form of policy measures intended to help correct the problem. Groups, such as the Alliance for Excellent Education, the Education Trust, *Education Week*'s Editorial

Projects in Education, and the Gates Foundation, have sponsored conferences, research, and programs and have published a multitude of articles intended to bring the problem to the forefront and encourage action. Losen (2008) described one early effort, jointly led by the Civil Rights Project, a think tank based at Harvard University, and Achieve, a nonprofit organization located in Washington, DC. The groups convened a conference in 2001 that Losen believes led to some provocative insights (Losen, 2008, p. 1):

> One of the more profound understandings to come from the conference was how little we knew about who was graduating from high school and who was dropping out. The research also revealed that the prevalent methods for estimating dropout and school completion rates were not very accurate, and likely underestimated the outcomes for minority dropout levels. A third revelation was that hundreds of schools, concentrated in the 35 largest cities in the U.S., graduated less than 50 percent of their freshman class.

Losen noted that, as a result of the increased attention to the dropout problem, findings from such efforts as the conference sponsored by the Civil Rights Project and Achieve, and intense lobbying by a number of groups, lawmakers addressed graduation rates in NCLB. At the time, efforts to hold schools and states accountable for student performance chiefly targeted improvements in achievement test scores. Some states and school districts had routinely provided estimates of their graduation and dropout rates, and the Goals 2000 Educate America Act called for increasing the graduation rate to 90 percent by 2000, but there were no previous mandates for reporting these rates or any common standards for such reports.

Initial NCLB Regulations

NCLB placed new emphasis on graduation rates, requiring that states report these rates as part of the adequate yearly progress (AYP) accountability measures. When the law passed, only 8 states collected data on graduation rates, and only 13 used those rates for accountability purposes (Swanson, 2004). This requirement was new to the states, and few had the data systems to support such calculations.

NCLB's guidance about graduation rates has changed over time and has not been entirely in line with the test-based accountability provisions in the law. According to Losen, the language signed into law defines graduation rates as "the percentage of students who graduate from secondary schools with a regular diploma in the standard number of years" (Losen, 2008). In guidance issued in May 2002, the U.S. Department of Education highlighted graduation as a performance goal for states, districts, and schools and called for the rates to be disaggregated by race, ethnicity, gender, disability status, migrant status, English proficiency status, and status as economically disadvantaged. However, when Secretary of Education Ronald Paige issued the final regulations, he said that graduation rates did not have to be disaggregated by minority subgroups for accountability purposes, except for the "safe harbor" provision.[3]

The dropout problem is considered by many to be a civil rights issue (Gutiérrez, 2008; Orfield, 2004), and reporting disaggregated rates is critical to revealing weak areas in the education system. As Maryland state legislator, Ana Sol Gutiérrez, put it at the workshop:

> Every year, across the country, . . . disproportionately high percentages of poor and minority students disappear from the educational pipeline before graduating from high school. . . . Because of misleading and inaccurate reporting of graduation rates, the public remains largely unaware of this educational and civil rights crisis.

Many advocacy groups found the regulatory guidance to be inadequate (Losen, 2008). They were particularly concerned that states and districts were not required to report graduation rates disaggregated for key groups of students and were not held accountable for their improvement.

Others were concerned because states were not required to set annual progress goals on graduation rates for their students, even for the aggregate of all students (Losen, 2008). The legislation had added graduation rates to the test-based measures of AYP required of each school and district, but the administration's regulations required yearly progress only for test scores. Accordingly, schools, districts, and states need only set a fixed goal for graduation rates, and it was up to the state to decide on the goal. Unlike the goals set for achievement test results, which require that 100 percent of students ultimately reach the proficient level, states could set much lower goals, even as low as 50 percent (Losen, 2008). Thus, while NCLB contained language intended to bring the dropout problem into the forefront, the regulatory guidance assigned it less priority than test-based progress indicators. Because the graduation rate provisions were so loosely defined, there were many concerns that the test-based mandates would lead schools to "push" low-performing students out of school in an effort to increase test scores.

A survey of the states conducted by the Civil Rights Project in fall 2003 revealed that no meaningful graduation rate accountability was in place. Only 10 states set a true floor for adequacy in graduation rates, whereby schools and districts that do not meet the state goals for 2 consecutive years are designated as having failed to make AYP. In 39 other states, falling short of the goal could be remedied by any improvement the following year (Losen, 2008). Other

---

[3]Safe harbor, as defined in Linn (2005, p. 7), means "if a subgroup of students in a school falls short of the adequate yearly progress (AYP) target, the school can still meet AYP if (a) the percentage of students who score below the proficient level is decreased by 10% from the year before, and (b) there is improvement for that subgroup on other indicators" (e.g., attendance rates, graduation rates).

reports further documented differences between the rates states reported to comply with NCLB and those estimated by Greene and others (e.g., Education Trust, 2003; Miao and Haney, 2004). These discrepancies spurred efforts to bring more uniformity to procedures for calculating the rates.

National Governors Association Compact

In 2005, the National Governors Association (NGA) formed the Task Force on State High School Graduation Data, charged with developing more accurate and consistent reporting of graduation rates. The NGA Compact, ultimately signed by all 50 governors, issued a set of five recommendations to help promote consistency in determining state graduation rates. Specifically (National Governors Association Task Force on State High School Graduation Data, 2005, pp. 7-8):

1. Immediately adopt, and begin taking steps to implement a standard 4-year adjusted cohort graduation rate (called the NGA graduation rate), as noted in equation 2.1:

$$\text{Grad rate} = \frac{\text{on-time graduates in year x}}{[\text{first-time entering 9th graders in year x} - 4] + (\text{transfers in}) - (\text{transfers out})} \qquad \text{(Eq. 2.1)}$$

2. Build the state's data system and capacity.
3. Adopt additional, complementary indicators to provide richer context and understanding about outcomes for students and how well the system is serving them.
4. Develop public understanding about the need for good graduation and dropout rate data.
5. Collaborate with local education leaders, higher education leaders, business leaders, and leaders of local community organizations.

These guidelines stimulated even greater awareness of the problem and paved the way for legislative change.

Initially, changes were evident at the state level. For instance, Gutiérrez described her efforts to have the NGA guidelines adopted by the state of Maryland. African American and Hispanic legislators in her state combined efforts to raise awareness about the problem. She highlighted for her colleagues the high cost to society of having such low graduation rates among poor and minority children, as well as the impact of having no standardized procedures for determining the extent of the problem. Her state enacted HB71 (2006), which requires the state education system to adopt and implement the NGA formula and to move toward establishing the needed tracking information systems.

Revised NCLB Regulations

In late October 2008, education secretary Margaret Spellings issued new NCLB regulations that established a uniform and comparable graduation rate. The regulations define a 4-year adjusted cohort graduation rate as "the number of students who graduate in 4 years with a regular high school diploma divided by the number of students who enter high school 4 years earlier, adjusting for transfers in and out, émigrés, and deceased students." The regulations go on to say:

> Students who graduate in four years include students who earn a regular high school diploma at the end of their fourth year, before the end of their fourth year, and, if the state so chooses, during a summer session immediately following their fourth year. (It does not include students who graduate with a modified diploma or certificate of attendance or through a General Educational Development [GED] program.) Students who graduate with a modified diploma or certificate of attendance or through a General Educational Development (GED) program are not included in the graduation rate.

The regulations also call for the state to establish a graduation rate goal that it expects all schools in the state to meet, to set annual graduation rate targets that reflect continuous and substantial improvement from the previous year, to report graduation rates disaggregated by subgroups, and to include the disaggregated rates in AYP determinations (http://www.ed.gov/policy/elsec/reg/proposal/uniform-grad-rate.html).

The rate called for by NCLB is generally in line with the rate endorsed by the NGA Compact. However, the NGA rate allows for modified diplomas (i.e., modified coursework and/or exit exams) and allows students with disabilities and English language learners extra time to graduate. Generally, the NGA rate leaves it to the state to determine which types of diplomas are counted in the rates and which are not, whereas the NCLB rate does not permit these flexibilities.

CONCLUSIONS AND RECOMMENDATIONS

Research findings document that there is a clear association between educational attainment and social and economic outcomes. The findings demonstrate that those with a high school diploma fare much better than those without. We find this evidence to be compelling: a high school diploma is essential for doing well in this country. We think that this research makes a strong case that all students need a high school diploma and that all schools should strive to ensure that all students complete the studies needed to earn this credential.

Public reporting of dropout and graduation rates is one way to bring attention to the problem and to identify schools and districts that need to make improvements. Requiring this reporting via accountability policy is one way to accomplish this. We therefore endorse the idea that accountability measures, such as NCLB, should require schools to report their graduation and dropout rates, both aggregated for the full population of students and disaggregated by race/ethnicity, gender, socioeconomic status, English language learner status, and disability status. We further think that schools and districts should report a number of different dropout and graduation rates and complementary indicators to provide a comprehensive and accurate understanding of the problem and their progress toward addressing it. Examples include graduation and completion rates for all entering ninth graders, regardless of whether they transfer, and grade 9 promotion rates.

Although public airing of rates brings attention to the problem, more is needed to enact the kinds of changes that need to occur. We think that schools should also be required to set progress goals for improving their completion rates and should be held accountable for achieving those goals.

The formulas that are adopted for these rates should be structured so that students who transfer from one school to another are included in the graduation and/or dropout rates for at least one school. The methods of including students in the formula should be designed to minimize the potential for introducing bias in the rates as a result of systematic transfers into or out of a school (an issue taken up in detail in Chapter 3).

We therefore recommend:

RECOMMENDATION 2-1: Federal and state accountability policy should require schools and districts to report a number of types of dropout, graduation, and completion rates: for all students and for students grouped by race/ethnicity, gender, socioeconomic status, English language learner status, and disability status. Furthermore, accountability policy should require schools and districts to set and meet meaningful progress goals for improving their graduation and dropout rates. Rates that are used for accountability should be carefully structured and reported in ways that minimize bias resulting from student mobility and subgroup definitions.

In calculating graduation and dropout rates for disaggregated groups of students, it is important to remember that trends in the rates are susceptible to change as a result of definitional criteria (an issue described further in Chapter 3). That is, the rates may fluctuate simply as a result of the definitions used or policy about who is included in the subgroup. To the extent possible, criteria for inclusion in subgroups should be made uniform across states and districts. To help users interpret these rates, information on the number of students in the subgroups should be included along with the reported rates.

As alluded to in this chapter, there are multiple ways to report these rates and a variety of decisions to make about how they are calculated. The remaining chapters of this report describe these issues.

3

Decisions Required to Compute the Indicators

Dropout and completion rates are among the most basic indicators of the effectiveness of a school, a school district, or a state education system. Although calculating the actual rates may seem simple, judgments must be made about who to include in the base group of students being tracked (i.e., the cohort), who to count as a graduate or a dropout, how many years to follow these students, and how to construct the formula. Each decision substantially affects the resulting rates. A number of reports have contrasted popular calculations in terms of their accuracy, bias, and ease of computation (e.g., Mishel and Roy, 2006; National Institute of Statistical Sciences and the Education Statistics Services Institute, 2005; Swanson, 2003; Warren, 2004). The technical definitional issues that are embedded in those calculations are at least as deterministic of bias and accuracy as the computations.[1]

Dropout and completion rates are based on a ratio, and one of the first decisions that needs to be made is how to define the numerator. Depending on the type of rate, the numerator represents dropouts, completers, or graduates. Identifying the students who are graduates is somewhat straightforward—they are the diploma earners. Identifying the students who fall into the other categories and distinguishing between graduates and other completers are more difficult. The second key decision is how to define the denominator, the full cohort of students with the potential of graduating or dropping out. Decisions

---

[1]Kaufman (2001), for example, found that differences in dropout and completion rates between the National Education Longitudinal Study and the Current Population Survey derived more from differences in definitions of populations and dropout/completion than from differences in their methods.

about how to include transfer students and students retained in grade in the cohort can have a major impact on its size and on the rate that is calculated.

At the workshop, Elaine Allensworth, with the Consortium on Chicago School Research, made a presentation about the kinds of decisions that must be made and the ways that they affect the calculation of the rates. This chapter is drawn from her paper (Allensworth, 2008).

DECISIONS AFFECTING THE NUMERATOR

Distinguishing Between Graduation and Completion

There is generally little ambiguity about who has obtained a high school diploma—lists of graduates must be maintained. However, there are multiple means of completing school besides earning a regular diploma, and not all students complete high school in the same time span. Accounting for different forms of completion has become increasingly complicated. In addition to granting diplomas, schools may offer programs that award General Educational Development (GED) credentials, or students may receive GEDs outside a K-12 school system.[2] Some districts offer alternative schools for students who have dropped out or are at risk of dropping out, and these schools may grant diplomas based on easier standards than the regular high school standards.[3] A number of states offer different levels of diplomas or grant certificates of attendance for students who do not pass state-required examinations or meet other criteria (Laird et al., 2008). Growth in home schooling and distance learning further complicates the ways in which completion is defined (National Institute of Statistical Sciences and the Education Statistics Services Institute, 2005).

There are a number of valid reasons for producing graduation rates that include only students who earn a regular high school diploma. There is little evidence that alternative methods of completion benefit most students who pursue these pathways to finishing high school. As noted in Chapter 1, GED recipients do not usually realize the same economic outcomes as high school graduates and are less likely to pursue higher education. Also, there is substantial variability across states and districts in the extent to which other forms of completion are available and recorded in an accessible manner.[4] Constraining

---

[2]Pallas (1989) provides a good description of the GED, as well as issues around alternative credentials and the different paths through which students may eventually obtain a diploma or credential or drop out.

[3]This is the case in Chicago, where alternative schools require students to complete the requirements set by the state for a diploma, rather than the much more demanding requirements set by the district.

[4]Data on alternative diplomas, GEDs, are not always recorded if provided by entities other than regular K-12 schools. This can be seen in the Common Core of Data, which allows three categories of completers to be reported (diploma recipients—included in the graduation rate, high school

completion rates to diploma recipients provides some degree of consistency across states and districts with different policies, programs, and data-recording procedures. It also helps maintain stability over time; that is, more comprehensive completion rates might increase over time simply because of an expansion in the availability of alternative forms of completion.[5] For purposes of accountability, counting only diploma recipients prevents perverse incentives for schools to push students out of regular programs into alternative or GED programs.

Constraining completion indicators to diploma recipients also has some shortcomings. Diploma requirements are not equivalent across states and districts, and they may change over time, making them not equivalent across different cohorts of students, even within the same school district.[6] In addition, when used for accountability, rates that include only graduates provide no incentive to districts to offer recovery programs for students not likely to obtain a regular diploma. Diploma-based rates also cannot be calculated for schools that offer alternative credentials, and thus, their effectiveness cannot be compared with schools that offer regular diplomas.

Timing of Completion

It may seem desirable to include all completers in the rate, regardless of how long it took them to complete their education. If the rates are being used as a tool to encourage good practices, it makes sense to allow a long time for completion so that schools do not have an incentive to give up on students who do not complete high school in four years. Time limitations for completion are problematic for students with disabilities: those whose Individualized Educational Plans (IEPs) specify that they remain in school beyond age 18 or who are ungraded and whose time in high school is not clearly defined. Time limitations may exclude summer graduates or students who take just one extra term to complete school. Practically, each extra year that is incorporated into the statistic means an additional year's wait before the completion rate can be reported. Whether the statistics are used for accountability, program evaluation, or assessment of the current state of educational attainment—it is generally critical to get timely information.

---

equivalency recipients, and other). The variability in defining completers is notable across states (Mishel and Roy, 2006).

[5]For example, based on the Common Core of Data, Warren (2005) noted a rise in regular diplomas in California from 1996 to 1997, but much less of a rise in the total number of high school completers—a fact he attributed to changes in how diplomas were classified.

[6]In recent years, many states have raised their graduation requirements or have developed plans to raise them. Currently, the standards for graduation vary widely across states. There are also different types of diplomas in some states, and some states allow parental waivers from the default curriculum (Achieve, Inc., 2008).

Time limits bring questions about how to count students still enrolled in school. Counting them as noncompleters maintains the definition as a four-year rate. However, this may not accurately represent the true state of high school graduation in the school or region. For instance, at the workshop, Mel Riddile, with the National Association of Secondary School Principals, noted that in some school districts, a student who does not graduate in June but finishes incomplete coursework over the summer, so that the diploma is awarded in July or August, is not always counted as a graduate in four-year rates. An alternative is to exclude students still enrolled from the indicator—removing them from both the numerator and the denominator. This allows the completion rate to be the opposite of the dropout rate, which is conceptually easier for a wide audience to understand. This also avoids any incentives to push out students who can no longer be counted as graduates. However, excluding large numbers of students from the calculation can be difficult to justify if there is concern that all students be counted. Furthermore, rates have the potential to be manipulated by delaying classification of students as dropouts.[7]

Distinguishing Between Dropouts and Transfers

Determining which students are dropouts is much more difficult than determining which students are graduates or completers. While students can graduate or complete a program only once, they can drop out of school repeatedly and from different school systems, making it difficult to know how to classify them at any given point in time.

Students who drop out often have high absentee rates. It is not always clear at which date these students should be considered dropouts, since they may have been absent for long periods of time before officially being dropped from the enrollment list. Some students never show up for high school. If a student finished grade 8 but does not officially enroll in high school, should the student be considered a dropout from the high school he or she never attended? The National Center for Education Statistics (NCES) requires schools to define enrollment on October 1. How are students classified if they leave grade 9 during September, after less than a month of school?

It is challenging to track down students who simply stop showing up at school. The student may have transferred to another school system, but verifying the transfer is difficult and requires administrative resources. Schools may miscode dropouts as transfers, even though their status is actually unknown,

---

[7]It may also, potentially, give a more accurate picture of the percentage of students who eventually graduate—if the same percentage of students remaining in school eventually graduate, something that can be tested empirically. In Chicago, this is the case, and excluding students still enrolled after four years produces rates that are similar to those that would be produced if students were allowed extra years to graduate.

a practice that leads to underestimates of the true dropout rate. Of particular concern is the way that schools code students who leave school to pursue a GED credential. Some may miscode them as transfers, particularly if they leave to enroll in a GED-granting institution, and as a result may eliminate them from both the numerator and the denominator when calculating rates, a practice that also leads to underestimates of the true dropout rate. Generally, students who leave school to pursue a GED credential should only be considered as transfers if they enroll in a program that grants diplomas (and in this case removed from the denominator of the rates). This tendency may be more prevalent when the rates are used for accountability purposes. For this reason, the National Forum on Education Statistics (2005) encourages states to require validation of transfers to verify (usually through a transcript request) that the student has enrolled in another school that grants regular diplomas.

Policies that require unverified student leavers to be coded as dropouts provide a substantial incentive for schools to obtain valid records of transfers. However, validation costs money,[8] and schools that have the greatest demand for validation of transfers—those with large numbers of mobile students—may not have the necessary resources. In general, requiring validation will inflate dropout rates and decrease completion rates, because students will be classified as dropouts until their transfer status can be verified. For instance, at the workshop, Rob Curtin, with the Massachusetts Department of Education, described a policy change in his state that required that all students coded as in-state transfers to be verified or, if unverified, to be coded as dropouts. This policy change produced a half-percent increase in the dropout rate in the first year it was implemented. Statewide data systems with individual student identifiers are useful for in-state validation, but they do not remedy the problem for across-state and out-of-country transfers.

Another issue is how to classify students who are incarcerated or otherwise institutionalized. It may seem logical to classify these students as transfers since the decision to leave their school was not voluntary, and the receiving institutions should provide them schooling. However, there is often no verification that incarcerated students are enrolled in a program leading to an accredited high school diploma or that they plan to re-enroll in a regular high school when released. Therefore, they are sometimes counted as dropouts, unless they re-enroll in school within the time frame being studied.

Finally, decisions must be made about how to classify students whose leave status changes over time. There are many potential paths to eventually becoming a dropout or a completer (Pallas, 1989). Most problematic is that students who have already been counted as dropouts may re-enroll and drop

---

[8]For a discussion of some of the issues around validation and data requirements, see the final report of the National Institute of Statistical Sciences and the Education Statistics Services Institute's (2005, Chapter 6 and Appendix D) task force on graduation, completion, and dropout indicators.

out a second or third time. For instance, at the workshop, Robin Taylor, with the Delaware Department of Education, reported that in her state 3 percent of the dropouts left school multiple times.

It is also unclear how to count dropouts who have re-enrolled in a different school or entered a school system through an alternative school. Since they enrolled as dropouts from another place, it may not be fair to the receiving school to count them as regular transfers into the new school or system. Problems of re-enrollment overlap with issues of transfer between schools, and the ways in which they can be handled depend on the way that the group or cohort being measured is defined in the first place.

DECISIONS AFFECTING THE DENOMINATOR

Defining the Base Grade of the Cohort

The cohort represented by dropout and completion indicators is almost always defined by grade, such as students entering grade 9 for completion statistics and students in grades 9-12 for dropout statistics. One complication posed by defining the base group by grade level is that students repeat grades. Grade 9, in particular, is frequently repeated, particularly by students who eventually drop out.[9] Thus, statistics defined by grade level often double- or triple-count students in rates representing different cohorts or years, and the students who are double-counted are those who are least likely to complete school. If students who are repeating a grade are not removed from the calculations, the statistics will be biased against schools with high levels of grade repetition. Because these schools are also likely to have high dropout rates, this accentuates the real differences in dropout/completion rates across schools and can make issues of equity appear more extreme than they really are (Mishel and Roy, 2006; Warren, 2004).

Even grade retention prior to high school can introduce problems in calculating the rates because a student's probability of dropping out is highly correlated with age.[10] If larger numbers of students enter high school at age 16 than in the past, dropout rates will rise simply because a larger percentage of the students are at an age when they are permitted to drop out. These age

---

[9]This can be seen, for example, in Abrams and Haney (2004), Nield and Farley (2004), and Allensworth and Easton (2005).

[10]For example, dropping out becomes legal at age 16, pregnancy becomes more likely at older ages, and full-time employment becomes more feasible as students get older. Data from Chicago show a positive relationship between grade level and the probability of dropping out, but it exists only because of the relationship between age and grade level. Holding age constant, there is no positive relationship between grade level and dropping out (the relationship becomes negative because of grade retention effects). Holding grade level constant, there is still a strong positive relationship between age and dropping out.

effects occur beyond any effects of grade retention, which itself increases the probability of eventually dropping out of school (Alexander, Entwisle, and Dauber, 2003; Allensworth, 2005a).

Changes in grade retention patterns prior to high school can also affect the comparability of grade 9 cohorts over time by delaying the entry of the academically weakest students. If larger numbers of students are retained in elementary school one year (e.g., because of the implementation of promotion standards), the dropout rate for one freshman cohort may improve simply because many of the cohort's low-achieving students have been moved into the next cohort. These kinds of policies affect the comparability of grade-based cohort rates over time and over cohorts.

Schools that have unusual grade configurations may not always be included in rates that define cohorts by grade. For example, middle schools that contain grade 9 but not grade 12 would not produce a graduation rate, even though they have a full grade 9 class. Incorporating ungraded special education students into grade-based cohorts is also problematic.[11]

One way to deal with these issues is to define cohorts by age instead of grade level. Age-based cohorts are not affected by patterns of grade retention in years prior to or during high school. This makes the rates more sensitive, accurate, stable, and unbiased than when the cohort is defined by grade level. In addition, students who never make it to high school can be included in the rates with their age peers, allowing the statistics to include middle grade dropouts. Special education students can also be included with their age peers, even if they are in ungraded classrooms. For districts and states, age-based rates can be more useful than grade-based rates to gauge trends over time and to assess the current state of education. However, they are not useful as indicators of school performance, since schools, parents, and the public generally want to know how many of the students who attend a school in a given year graduate or drop out later.

Specifying Enrollment Timelines

Defining the cohort also requires consideration of when the student enrolled in school. Because students could enroll in a school after a set date or leave school before that date, it is more inclusive to define the group as including any student enrolled over the period of a year (e.g., from October 1 of one year to September 30 of the next year) than to choose one date in the year for the base enrollment (e.g., enrolled by the 30th day of school). Most often, schools define school year enrollment from either October to October

---

[11]NCES includes ungraded students by prorating the total number across grades in the denominator proportional to known graded enrollment rates, with ungraded dropouts included in the numerator (Laird et al., 2008).

or June to June. Choosing one over the other has little effect on the resulting rates, but it does affect their interpretation—as students who dropped out in the school year versus students who were enrolled one year and did not return by the second year.[12]

Indicators that base their denominator on students enrolled on a specific date are particularly susceptible to undercounting students who transfer between schools. Those that compare the number of dropouts or completers over a set period (e.g., the school year, the next four years) to the enrollment at the set date will include students in the numerator who are not in the denominator. For instance, any student who enrolled in a school after the date that defined the cohort and then dropped out will be included in the numerator but not in the denominator. This leads to the potential for dropout rates that exceed 100 percent. In contrast, students could be included in the denominator who left the school soon after the cohort was defined and have no chance of being in the numerator, deflating the statistic.[13] If in- and out-mobility rates are similar, and if the students who leave have the same probability of completing/dropping out as the students who enter, then this does not result in bias or inaccuracy. However, these latter conditions do not always hold.

Adjustments can be made to account for in- and out-mobility so that the numerator remains a subset of the denominator. However, some of these adjustments require demographic assumptions that, if untrue, can introduce additional inaccuracy into the rates. Warren (2004) demonstrates how inaccuracies can be introduced when assumptions about in- and out-mobility, cohort size, and grade retention do not hold. In addition, adjustments that account for demographic instability must also assume that students who leave a school are similar to students who enter in terms of their probability of completion/dropout. This is often not the case when schools have different enrollment policies. If the students who leave a school are qualitatively different from the students who enter in a way that is systematically related to dropout/completion, the rates will be biased, even after adjustments are made to the denominator.

An alternative to defining the cohort on a specific date is to include all students enrolled at any time during the school year, or at any time over the four years of high school, for completion rates (with students entering at higher

---

[12]For the Common Core of Data dropout rates, some schools use the official October-to-October definition to define dropouts in the numerator, and some states use a June-to-June definition. Districts that use June-to-June dropout rates tend to report slightly higher numbers of dropouts, but the differences are small (Winglee et al., 2000).

[13]For instance, a student may be counted in the September enrollment but transfer in November. Unless adjustments are made for out-mobility, that student will be in the denominator of the indicator for the first school but will not be included in the numerator of the indicator for the first school. This will be true even if the student drops out in the spring, because the student's final status is known to the new school.

grades in each year after grade 9).[14] However, the data requirements are higher for this more inclusive definition; that is, schools must maintain individual-level records of students' dates of enrollment and departure. Furthermore, this definition results in students being counted at multiple institutions; if statistics are aggregated to higher level units (such as the district or state level), mobile students will be double-counted in the aggregate rates.

Decisions also must be made about whether to include students who are enrolled for a fraction of a year. Should schools be held responsible for students who enter and drop out within a week? If no minimum time period is set, including all students enrolled at a school in the denominator will generally increase dropout statistics because mobile students are more likely to drop out than other students. However, if a sizeable minimum time period is used to define who is a student (e.g., all students who enter after October 1 and remain through the end of the year), then dropout rates will be depressed, since, by definition, new students are included in the indicator only if they stay in school. In the end, issues of transfer and mobility are made no easier by including students enrolled over a period of time versus a snapshot; while the indicators are more inclusive, issues of aggregation and data requirements are more problematic.

Handling Transfer Students

When a student transfers between schools, it is not clear which unit should take responsibility for that student. In theory, there are four options: attribution to the receiving school, the sending school, both, or neither. In practice, schools tend to mix classification decisions depending on students' final status. For example, the graduation rate for the state of Illinois counts transfer students who graduate with their receiving school but those who drop out to neither school. Most of the graduation rates based on aggregate counts of students (including the Cumulative Proportion Index and the graduation rate in the Common Core of Data) attribute transfers who drop out to their sending school, but those who graduate to both schools—as a graduate at their receiving school and a nongraduate at their sending school. Mixing attribution inherently produces bias in the statistics.

Attribution to Both Schools

Counting students at both their sending and receiving schools is the most inclusive method for dealing with transfers. It ensures that all students are

---

[14]For example, students entering as grade 10 are grouped with students who started in grade 9 the year before; those entering as grade 11 are grouped with students who started grade 9 two years earlier, etc.

counted. However, it also ensures that transfer students will be counted at least twice—and more than twice for highly mobile students. This is problematic when school-level statistics are aggregated to produce district- or state-level rates because the mobile students (who are most at risk of dropping out) will be overcounted. Counting students at both schools also requires that schools share information or that information on graduation/dropout is maintained in a way that students' final status can be attributed to their first school.

An alternative might be to weight students' contribution to their school's rates by their time enrolled. This alternative is even more data intense, since it would require information about students' dates of entry and departure at each school to be available and shared between schools. It also would require strict guidelines for defining a dropout date for students with many absences to define the percentage of time enrolled at the final school. It is doubtful that such a method could be practically implemented.

Attribution to Neither School

Counting transfer students at neither the sending nor the receiving school has the obvious disadvantage of excluding all mobile students, which would produce an overly optimistic picture of the state of education at all levels of aggregation. This option eases calculation and data requirements, because no knowledge of final status is necessary. There are also political advantages, since schools do not feel they are being held accountable for problems created in other schools. In practice, only nongraduates are at risk of being excluded from the statistics of all schools—schools tend to want to count all of their graduates. This biases graduation rates upward, leading to more bias than if all transfer students were simply excluded.

Attribution to the Receiving School

Counting students with their final/receiving school makes practical sense because the final status is known to the school to which the student is attributed. It also makes intuitive sense to group students with the school from which they graduate or drop out. Schools generally feel that they should get credit for all of the students they graduate.

Although there are many practical advantages to counting transfers with their receiving school, doing so produces rates that are biased in favor of schools that can control their enrollment, and it can provide perverse incentives to transfer students at risk of not completing school. Attributing dropouts to their receiving school, instead of their sending school, assumes the problems that led students to drop out occurred at the final school. Yet, as discussed in Chapter 5, students' performance in their first year of high school is extremely predictive of eventual graduation (Allensworth and Easton, 2007). If a student leaves a school because of problems at that sending school, it may not be fair to credit that student's eventual withdrawal to the receiving school, especially if the student spent little time at the receiving school. This results in bias in the rates when schools have different enrollment policies. Schools that can choose whether to enroll a transfer student can boost their graduation rate by accepting students who have already shown some success in high school (e.g., on-time eleventh or twelfth graders).[15] This can happen, for example, if a school uses a lottery to pre-enroll eighth graders into grade 9 and then uses lotteries for grades 10-12; such a system precludes grade 9 repeaters. Likewise, schools with open enrollment can seem to be doing worse than they should since they accept students who have been unsuccessful in other places. This is a flaw inherent with the National Governors Association (NGA) graduation rate; it is biased in favor of schools that have some control over their enrollment.

Attribution to the Sending School

The final option is to count students with their first (sending) school. This is the method used for graduation rates at the college level in the NCES Graduation Rate Survey. Given the strong relationship between first-year course performance and eventual graduation, it makes sense from a conceptual standpoint to count students with their first school. It also prevents schools from benefiting by encouraging poorly performing students to transfer, particularly to schools that may not best serve their interests. It may seem unfair to count a student who transferred and then dropped out against the graduation rate of their original school. However, unless students are systematically leaving a school for a particular reason (e.g., because of safety concerns at the school that are forcing students out), the dropout and graduation rates of the school's former students should balance each other and not substantially affect the dropout rate. Using the first school also allows schools without a grade 12 (e.g., a middle school with grade 9) to be compared with other schools.

The problem with this approach is that students' final outcomes may not be known to the sending school. It can be done if student-level data are available at a district or state level, but there will still be out-of-district or out-of-state transfers that cannot be included in the calculations. The NCES college graduation rate circumvents this problem by counting all transfer students as nongraduates from their original college. This results in statistics that are unbiased and accurately represent the graduation rate of students who have matriculated at a given college, thus circumventing the problem of overcounting transfer students if statistics are aggregated. The disadvantage is that it underrepresents

---

[15]Students who transfer in after grade 9 tend to boost graduation rates because they have already shown enough success to move on past grade 9 and because they are followed for fewer years than students who enroll in grade 9.

the percentage of students who graduate overall; that is, it indicates only the percentage of students who graduate from their initial institution.

For purposes of accountability, this method does not produce perverse incentives to push students out of a school, but neither does it provide an incentive to ensure that students who transfer into a school are well served by the receiving school. Politically, it is difficult to convince schools that their graduates should not be counted in their completion indicators.

Choosing Among Methods

Each method of defining the numerator and denominator in a dropout/ completion statistic has advantages and disadvantages. No method will produce a statistic that is ideal for all purposes, and decisions about who to include or exclude will have an impact on the rate that is produced. Likewise, rules about who is included and excluded can produce incentives for school officials to act in ways that are not always in the best interest of students. For instance, a school can lower its dropout rate if it is allowed to classify students as transfers rather than dropouts when they leave school and enroll in a GED-granting program. A sole focus on the on-time (four-year) graduation rate can produce incentives for schools to push out students who are likely to take longer than four years to finish high school, particularly if they are allowed to remove these students from both the numerator and the denominator of the rate.

There are no optimal ways for handling these decisions that overcome all the potential disadvantages. However, steps can be taken to ensure that the impact of the decisions is understood. For instance, requiring school officials to document the status of transfer students and the decisions made in calculating the rates (i.e., who is included in the numerator and the denominator) is critical both for interpreting the rates and for revealing unintended incentives in the rules. Reporting a variety of rates—such as both on-time and eventual graduation rates, completion rates that include other methods of finishing high school, rates that do not remove transfer students or incorporate new students, and age-based rates—can provide a more comprehensive picture of schools' effectiveness at graduating students. Transparency with regard to the methodology underlying the statistics that are created and acknowledgment of their strengths and weaknesses is essential for understanding.

COMPUTING DISAGGREGATED RATES

Reporting disaggregated dropout and completion rates requires decisions about who should be included in each group. The No Child Left Behind (NCLB) Act requires schools to provide separate rates for students grouped by race/ethnicity, disability status, and English language proficiency. Yet it is not always clear who should be included in each group. For example, students can now self-identify their ethnicity and race using multiple categories (U.S. Department of Education, 2008), and students may change their race/ethnicity designation(s) from year to year. This can make classification difficult and inconsistent across schools. Changes in the ways students are classified result in rates that are not comparable over time, which can lead to false conclusions about the rates for particular groups.

English Language Learners

Calculating dropout and completion rates for English language learners (ELLs) is particularly difficult for a number of reasons. First, definitions of English proficiency are not always consistent across districts and states (Abedi and Dietel, 2004; National Research Council, 2004, in press). States have different criteria for initially classifying students as ELL and for reclassifying them (i.e., removing them from the ELL classification because they have acquired sufficient proficiency in English). This means that cross-state and/or cross-district comparisons of dropout and graduation rates for this subgroup may not be valid. More importantly, students' English proficiency status changes over time as they acquire sufficient English language skills to be removed from the ELL classification. Many students who are initially classified as ELL in the elementary grades are no longer classified as such in high school.

Students who are still classified as ELL in high school—the years when dropout and completion statistics are calculated—are generally a select group. They may be students who have had difficulty learning English and have remained in the classification longer than is typical. Or they may have been placed in the classification because they recently moved to the United States. Both of these factors are related to completing school. That is, students' rate of acquisition of English is correlated with their academic achievement and their socioeconomic status,[16] factors that are correlated with dropping out and completion. Immigration at older ages is also related to the likelihood of graduation, as children who move to the United States at older ages tend to obtain fewer years of education than children who immigrate when very young (Allensworth, 1997). Highly mobile students are also more likely to remain classified as ELL longer than students who are less mobile because they tend to have long periods of "service breaks" due to absence or transfer; mobility is another characteristic correlated with high school completion. For these reasons, students still in the bilingual or English as a second language program

---

[16]Hakuta, Butler, and Witt (2000) found that academic English proficiency takes at least four to seven years, and that the rate of acquisition is related to students' economic status. Abedi and Dietel (2004) note that high-performing English language learners get redesignated as they obtain proficiency. As a result, low-achieving students are increasingly concentrated in the subgroup, together with students newly classified as English language learners.

in high school would be expected to have higher dropout rates than students not in these programs.

In order to obtain the most accurate estimates of schools' success rates at graduating ELL students, it is essential to know which students have been classified as ELL at any time during their schooling, particularly during the primary grades. This requires data systems to include records on ELL status from the primary grades onward that remain constant as students progress to higher grades—a requirement not easily met, since many states do not have access to primary grade records for these students. These primary grade records would need to accompany students who transfer, so that receiving schools can correctly classify students who were formerly classified as ELL. Otherwise, statistics that are aggregated from school records will fail to include former ELL students who transferred out of their original school.

Students with Disabilities

Unlike ELL status, students' disability status does not typically change over time. That is, having a hearing, visual, emotional, or cognitive impairment or a learning disability is usually not a temporary condition. However, classification criteria for these students are not always consistent across schools, districts, or time (National Research Council, 2004), and thus their status as a recipient of special education services may change over time. The classification criteria depend, in part, on the resources available in the school and the district for diagnosis, as well as district policies about designating students as disabled.[17] Because the criteria for placing students into the category differ across schools and districts, the dropout and completion rates for this group of students may not be comparable across units.

Furthermore, students who have achievement well below grade level are sometimes classified as learning disabled simply on the basis of their low achievement, even though they may not meet the other criteria for the learning disability classification. These students may be low-achieving because they actually have a learning disability, or their low achievement may be due to other factors that are related to the likelihood of completion, such as years of low engagement in school. Classifying students into the group based on a

---

[17]Eligibility for special education services depends on referral, evaluation, and decisions of school staff and parents. These decisions may differ across schools. School policies and resources may affect whether students are referred or determined to be eligible. Chicago, for example, placed limits on the percentage of students who could be determined eligible for special education services, in part, to keep schools from excluding too many students from the accountability policy. When grade promotion policies were put into place in grades 3, 6, and 8, there was a substantial rise in the identification of students in those grades. This seemed to be due to uncertainty as to how to handle students whose achievement remained low after repeatedly failing the exams and being held back one or more years (Miller and Gladden, 2002).

characteristic (low achievement) that itself is highly correlated with dropping out can produce misleading results when the indicator is calculated. That is, the dropout/completion indicator may look worse for this group because it includes students who may not belong in the category and are at a higher risk of dropping out due to the characteristic that caused them to be placed in the category.

In addition, the time element in cohort/group definition is also particularly problematic for students with disabilities, as some of them are given more than four years to complete high school in their Individualized Education Plan or are to remain in the school system past age 18.

AGGREGATING RATES

An additional issue to consider when designing indicators is whether they will be aggregated to represent completion or dropout rates at higher levels of analysis. Rates that are accurately defined at the school level are subject to a number of errors when aggregated to the district, state, or federal level.[18] For instance, the ways that transfer students are handled can result in their being omitted or double-counted in aggregated rates. Having individual-level student data can alleviate these problems. However, subgroup definitions (e.g., defining who is an ELL student or a special education student) become more problematic at the state level, where there may be less detailed longitudinal information on individual students.

Students still enrolled after the date they should have graduated are often counted multiple times, particularly if the rates are calculated from aggregate numbers of students instead of longitudinal student records. They are initially counted as noncompleters in their own cohort; they are counted again in the cohort that follows, either as completers or noncompleters. This introduces inaccuracy in the rates, but whether they are inflated or deflated depends on the specific way in which students are double-counted and whether adjustments are made to the denominator along with the numerator. Incorporating students who remain in school an additional year also makes the indicator less sensitive to changes in dropout and completion that may be occurring in the school, which in turn makes them less useful for evaluating the effects of new policies and practices.

---

[18]For example, dropout rates in a district with two high schools might represent all students enrolled at each school over a period of four years. If there were high student mobility rates between the schools, so that many students transfer from one to the other, the resulting dropout rates for the schools would still be correct estimates of the percentage of students ever enrolled at those schools who dropped out. But the aggregate dropout rate for the district, based on an average of the two schools, would double-count students who had enrolled at each school. This would lead the district statistic to be inaccurate, even though based on accurate school statistics.

CONCLUSIONS AND RECOMMENDATIONS

Graduation and dropout rates are critical outcome measures of secondary schooling and should be incorporated into accountability systems. However, there are inherent weaknesses in any method of calculating those rates. Even the NGA graduation rate, which we encourage states to adopt, is biased in favor of schools that can control their enrollments. However, if the limitations of the calculations are made explicit, alternative rates could be calculated to verify any conclusions that are made with the statistics. For example, if charter schools were judged to be more effective at retaining students based on the NGA rate, it would be prudent to calculate alternative statistics not biased by school's enrollment policies to verify this conclusion. This would require data to be available to calculate the complementary statistics. Thus, it is important to produce other indicators of the outcomes of secondary schooling and the development of a robust data system that can produce different variations of the completion rate estimates.

To the greatest extent possible, the methods for computing the rates should meet the following criteria: (1) provide the most accurate assessment possible of how many students actually complete or drop out of school, (2) not be biased in favor of certain types of schools, (3) be inclusive of all students but not double-count them, (4) be stable enough to validly track trends over time, and (5) be sensitive to real changes in student outcomes. All of this must be done within the constraints of the data systems available to schools and given the purpose for which the statistics are to be used. No indicator is perfect, and trade-offs among the criteria are usually required. Ultimately, decisions about the indicators and the ways to calculate them should reflect the intended purpose and uses. The trade-offs, strengths, and shortcomings should be made explicit. We therefore recommend:

> **RECOMMENDATION 3-1:** The strengths and weaknesses of dropout and completion rates should be made explicit when the rates are reported.

> **RECOMMENDATION 3-2:** Rates should be accompanied with documentation about the underlying decisions that were made regarding students who transfer from one school to another, are retained in grade, receive a GED credential or an alternative diploma, and take longer than four years to graduate.

Because decisions about how to handle various groups of students can affect the rates, we think it is important to supplement dropout and completion indicators with information to help users accurately interpret them. As described in this chapter, schools and states have different policies for handling transfer students. Documentation of how transfers were handled is critical for interpreting school-level rates. Also useful is an estimate of the transfer/leave rate and supplementary graduation/dropout rates that do not remove transfers or incorporate new students. This additional information would allow examination of the ways in which schools' policies for handling transfer students affect the reported rates.

Policies for grade retention also vary across schools, districts, states, and time. These policies, and particularly year-to-year changes in these policies, can cause trends in the rates to fluctuate over time. Age-based cohort rates can provide information to help users understand and evaluate trends in grade-based rates. Age-based rates have the advantage that they are unaffected by patterns in grade retention that may have affected one cohort differentially from another. They are also more inclusive, in that they can include students who never make it to high school and can include special education students with their peers. If the limitations associated with a reported rate are made explicit, supplemental rates can be calculated to verify any conclusions that are based on the statistics, although this would require data to be available to calculate the supplemental statistics. We therefore recommend:

> **RECOMMENDATION 3-3:** To the extent possible, data should be made available to allow supplementary rates to be calculated that compensate for the limitations in reported rates and help users to further understand the rates. Types of supplementary information include transfer rates, rates that do not remove transfer students or incorporate new students, age-based rates, and the percentage of students with unknown graduation status.

The federal government requires states and districts to produce 4-year graduation rates that include diploma recipients only. As discussed above, there are compelling reasons for using this statistic as the primary indicator of high school completion. However, there are also legitimate reasons to produce more inclusive completion indicators that allow students more time to complete high school and include other forms of completion, such as GEDs and alternative diplomas. Unless there is a common definition, such statistics will not be comparable across districts and states and over time. We therefore recommend:

> **RECOMMENDATION 3-4:** In addition to the standard graduation rate that is limited to 4-year recipients of regular diplomas, states and districts should produce a comprehensive completion rate that includes all forms of completion and allows students up to six years for completion. This should be used as a supplemental indicator to the 4-year graduation rate, which should continue to be used as the primary indicator for gauging school, district, and state performance.

As part of the NCLB regulations, states and districts are expected to report disaggregated graduation rates, such as for students grouped by low-income eligibility, disability status, and English language learner status, and to track their progress over time. These subgroup statistics are often not comparable across schools, districts, or states due to differing methods and rates of identification and reclassification into and out of the subgroup. Furthermore, the methods by which students are placed into subgroups can lead to inaccurate judgments about educational efficacy in a school system for members of the subgroup. For English language learners, inaccuracies are introduced because classification into the subgroup changes over time, and the rate of reclassification is correlated with dropping out. For students with disabilities, underidentification of disabilities and different methods of classifying disabilities result in lack of comparability. Furthermore, because some students with disabilities are expected to remain in school for more than four years, the subgroup statistics for students with disabilities will disproportionately be affected by decisions about the number of years allowed for graduation in the indicators (e.g., four-year versus five-year rates).

The main purpose of subgroup statistics is to gauge the degree to which schools, districts, and states are serving particular groups of students. To make these judgments fairly, alternative statistics should provide supplemental information for subgroups. With regard to graduation rates for these subgroups, we recommend:

> **RECOMMENDATION 3-5:** To improve knowledge about graduation rates among subgroups, alternate statistics should complement conventional indicators. Alternative graduation rates for English language learners (ELLs) should include former ELL students as well as students currently classified in this category. Thus, records on ELL status should accompany students as they progress through grades, change ELL status, and transfer across districts. Alternative graduation rates for special education students and English language learners should allow additional years toward graduation.

4

Current and Proposed Measures

What was the high school dropout rate last year? What was the graduation rate? Most people believe that quantifying these rates should be a straightforward task. Intuitively, it might seem that calculating the dropout rate simply means dividing the number of students who drop out by the total number of students in the cohort and, similarly, that calculating the graduation rate simply means dividing the number of students who graduate by the total number in the cohort. Intuitively, it might also seem that once one of the rates is obtained, the other can be calculated by subtracting it from 100.

As those who work in this area can attest, calculating the rates is not that simple. The rates can be calculated from a variety of different data sources using a variety of different methods. These differences can lead to discrepant estimates of the rates. For instance, consider the high school completion rates published for the 2005-06 school year. The U.S. Department of Education reported that approximately 73 percent of public high school students graduated on time that year (Snyder, Dillow, and Hoffman, 2009, p. 3), and Editorial Projects in Education (2008, p. 28) reported a similar figure of 69 percent. However, the U.S. Department of Education also reported a dropout rate for 16- to 24-year-olds of only 9 percent in 2006 (Snyder, Dillow, and Hoffman, 2009, Table 105), and the Annie E. Casey Foundation (2009, p. 64) reported a dropout rate for 16- to 19-year- olds of only 7 percent. How should a completion rate of between 69 and 73 percent be interpreted in light of a dropout rate below 10 percent?

Why do estimates of the high school completion rate and the high school dropout rate differ so much from one another? How can these disparate estimates be reconciled? The disparities can be traced to three sources:

(1) differences in what various estimates are designed to accomplish, (2) differences in the conceptual and technical definition of both the numerator and the denominator used to calculate the rates, and (3) differences in the accuracy of the data used to produce them. Understanding these three sources of differences is key to making sense of the resulting rates.

This chapter first discusses the different purposes of the estimates and the sources of data used in calculating the rates. We then discuss the different types of rates that can be calculated. We close the chapter by discussing the importance of aligning the choice of a rate with the purpose it will serve. The chapter draws extensively from papers prepared for the workshop by Rob Warren, with the University of Minnesota, and Elaine Allensworth, with the Consortium on Chicago School Research (Allensworth, 2008; Warren, 2008).

DIFFERENT PURPOSES OF THE ESTIMATES

One major source of differences in estimates of dropout and completion rates is the question they were designed to answer. Analysts operationalize high school completion and dropout rates in different ways because they have different conceptual or practical reasons for making those measurements. There are three chief uses of high school completion and dropout rates.

The first use is to describe the amount (or lack) of human capital in a population. In this case, the rates characterize an attribute of society: they quantify the share of people who bring particular credentials and skills to the labor force. The second use is to describe the "holding power" of schools. In this case, the rates answer questions about schools; they characterize their success at moving young people from the first day of high school to successful completion (see Hartzell, McKay, and Frymier, 1992). The third use is to describe students' success at navigating high school from beginning to end. For this purpose, the rates answer questions about individual students themselves; they measure how successful students are in progressing from the first day of high school to successful completion.

If the goal of the rate is to describe the amounts of human capital in a population, the timing of high school completion—how long ago or at what age people completed high school—is not of critical importance. Nor, for some purposes, does it matter exactly how young people complete high school—by obtaining a diploma, a General Educational Development (GED) credential, or a certificate of completion, completing an adult education program, or some other way. For other purposes, however, how students complete high school is critical because research suggests that students who fail to earn a regular high school diploma are less competitive in the labor market compared with graduates (Heckman and Rubinstein, 2001; Tyler, 2003). Any young person who has completed high school is considered to have acquired marketable capital, regardless of his or her age at the time of crossing that educational threshold.

For the latter two uses, however, both the timing of high school completion and the manner in which young people complete high school can be important. For instance, schools may be deemed successful at moving young people through to completion only if they obtain regular diplomas "on time," typically within four years.

Given these differences in intended purpose, it becomes less puzzling to read in the *Digest of Education Statistics* that "73.4 percent of public high school students graduated on time," despite the fact that only 9 percent of 16- to 24-year-olds were dropouts in 2006 (Snyder, Dillow, and Hoffman, 2009, p. 3 and Table 109). The former estimate is explicitly intended to describe the share of a cohort of students that has completed high school on time and by obtaining a diploma—essentially an attribute of schools. The latter estimate is clearly intended to describe the share of young people who are not gaining the human capital associated with high school completion. Presumably many of the 26.6 percent of ninth graders in fall 2002 who did not go on to graduate from high school with a diploma by spring 2006 were still enrolled or will compete high school later, via a GED or another alternative credential.[1] Given the reported 9 percent dropout rate, one might presume that eventually about 91 percent of young people will eventually complete high school one way or another.[2]

DIFFERENT DATA SOURCES

Another source of differences in the rates is the data used in the calculations. A number of available data sources can be used for calculating the rates. These data were collected for different reasons using different types of designs—cross-sectional sample surveys, longitudinal sample surveys, cross-sectional administrative data, and longitudinal administrative data. The collection method and the reasons for collecting the data can affect the rates that are calculated. In this section, we describe the major data sources used in this country to compute high school dropout and completion rates and discuss their strengths and weaknesses in relation to the three purposes listed above.

Cross-Sectional Sample Surveys

The data most widely used for measuring high school dropout and completion come from the Current Population Survey (CPS),[3] the U.S. decennial

---

[1] 100 percent − 73.4 percent = 26.6 percent.

[2] 100 percent − 9 percent = 91 percent.

[3] Technically, CPS data are not cross-sectional, although they are often used as if they were. That is, if a subject is selected to respond to the CPS, the person is surveyed 8 times over 16 months, which makes the data longitudinal. Using the data longitudinally is technically very difficult, so they are rarely used in this way. We think this has contributed to the misconception that the data are cross-sectional rather than longitudinal.

census, and (in more recent years) the American Community Survey (ACS). Because the census is conducted every 10 years and the ACS is a relatively new resource, the CPS has served as the central cross-sectional data resource for decades.[4]

The CPS is conducted monthly by the Census Bureau for the Bureau of Labor Statistics and surveys more than 50,000 households. Households are selected in such a way that it is possible to generalize to the nation as a whole and, in recent years, to individual states and other specific geographic areas. Individuals in the CPS are broadly representative of the civilian, noninstitutionalized population of the United States. In addition to the basic demographic and labor force questions that are included in each monthly administration of the CPS, questions on selected topics are included in most months. Since 1968, the October CPS has obtained basic monthly data as well as information about school enrollment—including current enrollment status, public versus private school enrollment, grade attending if enrolled, most recent year of enrollment, enrollment status in the preceding October, grade of enrollment in the preceding October, and high school completion status. In recent years, the October CPS has also ascertained whether high school completers earned diplomas or GED certificates.

There are a number of conceptual and technical problems with CPS-derived measures of high school dropout and completion, particularly when computed at the state level. Most importantly, the sample sizes are not large enough to produce reliable estimates of rates of high school completion or dropout at the state or substate levels (Kaufman, 2001; Winglee et al., 2000). Even when data are aggregated across years—for instance, in the Annie E. Casey Foundation's *Kids Count* (2008) measure—the standard errors of estimates for some states are frequently so large that it is difficult to make meaningful comparisons across states or over time. Moreover, when aggregated across years, the resulting measure does not pertain to specific cohorts, and because the CPS data are typically tabulated by age rather than grade level, they usually do not pertain to specific cohorts of incoming students. As a result, CPS-based measures are not useful, except at the national level and possibly aggregated across survey years, for assessing schools' holding power or for describing the dropout or completion rates of school entry cohorts.

Second, until 1987, it was not possible to distinguish high school completers from GED recipients in the CPS. Since 1988, October CPS respondents who recently completed high school have been asked whether they obtained a diploma or a GED, but there are serious concerns about the quality of the resulting data (Chaplin, 2002; Kaufman, 2001). Third, as noted by Greene and Forster (2003), "[status] dropout statistics derived from the [CPS] are

---

[4]In 2008, the Census Bureau began collecting educational attainment data as part of the ACS, which has broader population coverage and provides data for smaller geographic areas than the CPS.

based on young people who live in an area but who may not have gone to high school in that area." To the extent that young people move from state to state after age 18, estimates of state high school dropout rates based on CPS data—particularly status dropout rates based on 16- to 24-year-olds—may be of questionable validity (see also Kaufman, McMillen, and Bradby, 1992).

Fourth, there are concerns about population coverage with the CPS, particularly for racial/ethnic minorities. The CPS is representative of the civilian, noninstitutionalized population of household residents in the United States, so young people who are incarcerated, in the military, or homeless are not represented. To the extent that these populations differ from the rest of the population with respect to frequency and method of high school completion, there is the potential for CPS-based estimates to differ from those based on other data sets that capture these populations. Finally, substantial changes over time in CPS questionnaire design, administration, and survey items have made year-to-year comparisons difficult (Hauser, 1997; Kaufman, 2001).

It is possible to overcome some, but not all, of these limitations of the CPS by using data from the ACS or the decennial census. Sample sizes are larger, enhancing the reliability of state- and urban-level estimates. Both the ACS and the decennial census include individuals who are institutionalized or in the military, which enhances the generalizability of the reported statistics. However, it is still not clear how accurately ACS respondents report whether they obtained GEDs or regular high school diplomas.

In addition, the ACS and the decennial census share with the CPS the limitation that sampled young people are not asked to indicate the state(s) in which they attended high school or the school they attended. As a result, the ACS and the census are useful for constructing rates that describe the human capital of populations; however, measures derived from the CPS, the ACS, and the census are not well suited to describing schools' holding power, because they never refer to specific schools at all, or to young people's success in navigating the secondary school system.

Longitudinal Sample Surveys

Although a number of longitudinal sample surveys are used for constructing dropout and completion rates (e.g., the National Longitudinal Surveys), the most widely used are those conducted periodically by the Bureau of Labor Statistics (see http://www.bls.gov/nls/) and the National Center for Education Statistics (NCES) (see http://nces.ed.gov/surveys/SurveyGroups. asp?group=1). The NCES surveys include the following:

- The 1972 sample of seniors in the National Longitudinal Study of the High School Class of 1972 (NLS).

- The 1980 and 1982 samples of sophomores and seniors in High School & Beyond (HS&B).
- The sample of eighth graders in the 1988 National Educational Longitudinal Study (NELS).
- The sample of sophomores in the 2002 Educational Longitudinal Study (ELS).

Of these four data sources, NELS has been at the center of a great deal of research and debate on the measurement of high school dropout and completion rates in recent years (e.g., see Greene, Winters, and Swanson, 2006; Kaufman, 2004; Mishel, 2006; Mishel and Roy, 2006). Thus, we focus on NELS in the discussion below.

NELS is a longitudinal survey of the grade 8 student cohort of 1988. In the base year, the sample included approximately 25,000 randomly selected students in 1,000 public and private schools across the United States. In addition to the data collected from student interviews, NELS contains information from parents, school administrators, teachers, and student transcripts. The initial student cohort has been resurveyed on four occasions, in 1990, 1992, 1994, and 2000. Students who dropped out of school between surveys were also interviewed. In the early follow-up surveys, the sample was "freshened" with new sample members in order to make the first and second follow-up surveys cross-sectionally representative of 1990 sophomores and 1992 seniors, respectively. The content of the surveys includes students' school, work, and home experiences; educational resources and support; parental and peer influences; educational and occupational plans and aspirations; delinquency; and many others (Curtin et al., 2002).

For the purposes of measuring high school dropout and completion rates, the key feature of NELS (and of other longitudinal sample surveys as well) is that it includes information about whether and when cohort members dropped out of school and whether and how they obtained secondary school credentials. A key design feature of NELS is the availability of transcript data on high school enrollment, dropout, and completion. In the absence of coverage bias and nonparticipation, NELS data would provide very accurate estimates of high school dropout and completion rates at the national (but not state or district) level—albeit for a single cohort of young people.

Despite the advantages associated with its longitudinal design, a number of technical issues raise questions about the accuracy of dropout and completion rates based on NELS (Kaufman, 2004); these issues also arise in the context of other longitudinal surveys based on samples. First, the base-year NELS sample excluded many students with limited English proficiency or mental or physical disabilities. NCES gathered supplementary information from these students later, but it is not clear how often this supplemental information is used in calculating NELS-based dropout and completion rates. Second, as noted by

Kaufman (2004, p. 119), "[s]ince NELS is a sample survey, it is subject to the same potential for bias due to non-response and undercoverage that CPS has." Third, transcript data are frequently unavailable for dropouts or alternative completers. This is due in part to the logistical difficulties inherent in collecting such data and in part to nonresponse by schools (Ingels et al., 1995). Some of these problems are overcome by the use of sample weights in NELS; nevertheless, NELS—like all longitudinal sample surveys—has a difficult time retaining hard-to-follow individuals like high school dropouts.

Administrative Data

Each state maintains its own system for counting the numbers of students who are enrolled in each grade (usually at the beginning of each academic year), the numbers of students who drop out of school, and the numbers of students who obtain regular diplomas and other high school completion credentials. These counts are usually aggregated up from the schoolhouse level, and they are increasingly linked to longitudinal data systems. At the national level, cross-sectional administrative data on enrollments and numbers of completers are compiled as part of the Common Core of Data (CCD).

Compiled by NCES, the CCD is the federal government's primary database on public elementary and secondary education. Each year the CCD survey collects information about all public elementary and secondary schools from local and state education agencies. One component of the CCD—the State Nonfiscal Survey—provides basic, annual information on public elementary and secondary school students and staff for each state and the District of Columbia. The State Nonfiscal Survey includes counts of the number of students enrolled in each grade in the fall of each academic year as well as the number of students who earned regular diplomas, earned other diplomas, or completed high school in some other manner in the spring of each academic year. Although the State Nonfiscal Survey has collected counts of public school dropouts since the 1991-92 school year, many states have not provided this information or have provided it in a manner inconsistent with the standard CCD definition of dropout (Winglee et al., 2000; Young and Hoffman, 2002).

One obvious limitation of CCD data—and indeed of all state administrative data—is that they pertain exclusively to public school students. When high school dropout and completion rates are used for the purposes of describing levels of human capital in a population or for describing young people's success at navigating the secondary education system, this limitation is important. In 2009, 8.4 percent of secondary school students were enrolled in private schools (Snyder and Dillow, 2010, Table 55), which gives a sense of the extent of the population not represented by CCD and state administrative data.[5] The CCD

---

[5] One national survey is available that collects data from private schools. Results from this survey

is also limited because it excludes secondary credentials awarded outside the K-12 education system, such as Adult Education and Jobs Corps.[6]

Beyond these cross-sectional, state-produced enrollment counts, states also frequently make use of longitudinal administrative data to produce high school dropout and completion rates. Each state uses somewhat different procedures for data collecting, reporting, and aggregation, but in general there have been few concerns about states' reports of the numbers of students in each grade or the numbers of students obtaining regular diplomas. The most prominent controversies pertain to decisions about how to handle the data. For instance, although there is little concern about states' abilities to accurately count the number of students who begin high school as ninth graders, there is frequently concern about how states account for factors like migration, incarceration, expulsion, and enrollment in alternative educational programs.

DIFFERENT TYPES OF RATES

There is no one best measure of high school dropout or completion. Different methods of calculating graduation, completion, and dropout rates will be more or less useful for different purposes and more or less valid and reliable for different types of students (National Institute of Statistical Sciences and the Education Statistics Services Institute, 2005; Swanson, 2003). Below we discuss three types of rates: status rates, event rates, and cohort rates.[7] We distinguish between cohort rates based on individual data (which we refer to as "individual cohort rates") and cohort rates based on aggregated data (which we refer to as "aggregate cohort rates").

Status Rates

A status rate reports the fraction of a population that falls into a certain category at a given point in time. The most common example is the status dropout rate, although status enrollment rates and status completion rates are also occasionally reported. For instance, in *Dropout Rates in the United States, 2006* the U.S. Department of Education reported that 9.3 percent of 16- to 24-year-olds were not enrolled in school and did not have any high school credential in October of that year (Laird et al., 2008). In that same month, 87.8 percent

---

have been used in conjunction with the CCD to calculate national graduation rates. See Chaplin and Klasik (2006) at http://www.uark.edu/ua/der/EWPA/Research/Accountability/1790.html.

[6]Adult Education, for example, awarded 62,598 diplomas and equivalency credentials in 2008-09 (data retrieved July 19, 2010, from http://wdcrobcolp01.ed.gov/CFAPPS/OVAE/NRS/reports/index.cfm).

[7]See also National Institute of Statistical Sciences and the Education Statistics Services Institute (2005) for a more technical description of the various types of rates.

of 16- to 24-year-olds were status completers; that is, they were not enrolled in high school and held some sort of high school credential.

The numerator of the status dropout rate reflects the number of people who have not obtained any high school credential and are not working toward one. The fact that many dropouts subsequently re-enroll in high school, obtain a GED credential, or earn high school credentials in other ways is immaterial in calculating the rate, as is the age at which young people complete high school.

Status dropout and completion rates are usually calculated using cross-sectional data on individuals in the target population. All that is required is information about individuals' ages, enrollment status,[8] and high school completion status. All status dropout and completion rates are measures of the amount (or lack) of human capital in a population. Status rates do not differentiate between those with a diploma and those with a GED or other credentials, however, and do not consider when the credential was earned. As such, they are poor measures of schools' holding power or of young people's success at navigating the secondary school system and persisting in school. A low status dropout rate may reflect very high holding power of schools, or it may obscure a situation in which schools have very low holding power and many young people obtain alternate credentials in their late teens or early twenties.

Moreover, status rates do not account for the location of schools. A geographic area may have a low status dropout rate because its schools have high holding power, or the area may attract people who have high school credentials. For instance, counties with high technology industries or large postsecondary institutions tend to have relatively low status dropout rates. This probably says more about the human capital of people who move to those counties than about the holding power of the schools there.

Event Rates

An event rate reports the fraction of a population that experiences a particular event over a given time interval; by definition, everyone in the population is at risk of experiencing that event during the period. The most frequently reported example is the event dropout rate—the proportion of students who exit school during a given academic year without completing high school.

Event dropout and completion rates can be calculated using either cross-sectional or longitudinal data. All that is required is information about individuals' enrollment status in two consecutive academic years, their completion status in the second of those years, and (under some formulations) age. Enrollment status is typically measured at the beginning of each academic year

---

[8]It is important to note that enrollment status can be a problematic concept, in that individuals may be enrolled full-time or part-time and in a regular school, a continuation school, or night school.

so the rate can more clearly represent the incidence of dropping out during a well-defined period of time.

For instance, Kominski (1990) developed an event dropout rate that could be calculated from data collected in the October School Enrollment Supplement of the Current Population Survey; that rate could be estimated separately at grades 10, 11, and 12 or combined across all three grade levels. Research on national trends and differentials in the event dropout rate was undertaken by Hauser (1997) and by Hauser, Simmons, and Pager (2004). The rates estimated in those studies fall well below those of the more extreme (high) estimates of status dropout and, perhaps partly for that reason, have received little public attention. Misinterpretation of event rates as cohort rates often leads people to believe that dropout rates are lower than they really are. Because event rates are sometimes reported for students at all grade levels and ages, who have very different risks of dropout, and because the CPS provides very small samples at the relevant ages, they are rarely sufficiently sensitive for gauging the effects of changes in school practices, even at the state or regional level. Another disadvantage of this rate, shared by the status dropout rate when estimated from the CPS, is that it excludes those in the institutionalized population, such as students in prison or in the military. There are also population coverage problems in the CPS, especially for minorities.

Because they are measures of the share of a population that experiences a particular event over the course of a specific time interval, event dropout and completion rates can be used to describe schools' holding power or young people's ability to successfully navigate the school system. Whether an event dropout rate is a fair characterization depends on (a) how "success" and "failure" are defined in the numerator and (b) how the population is defined in the denominator. If the goal is to measure schools' holding power, the numerator is determined by how schools define success (e.g., they are explicit about whether GEDs and other alternative credentials are treated as equivalent to regular diplomas), and the denominator is restricted to those continuously residing in a well-defined geographic area (typically a school district or state). The resulting event dropout rate thus describes the experiences of only those students for whom the school district or state is formally responsible. If the goal is to measure the rate at which students' succeed in navigating the secondary school system, the denominator need not be restricted to those who continuously reside in a particular geographic area.

Individual Cohort Rates

Individual cohort rates are derived from longitudinal (or retrospective) data on individuals, all of whom were the same age or in the same grade at a certain point in time (e.g., students entering high school in a given year). Individual cohort rates report the fraction of individuals who transition into a particular status (e.g., dropouts, graduates, completers) by a subsequent point in time, typically within four years.

There are two general sources for the longitudinal data used to compute cohort dropout and completion rates. The first source is administrative data collected by the school system, district, and/or state. In this case, the number of first-time ninth graders in the fall of a given academic year is the denominator for the rate. Depending on the kind of rate desired, the numerator is formed by counting the number of students who obtain diplomas (for graduation rates), obtain any secondary credential (for completion rates), or leave school without obtaining any credential (for dropout rates). As with event dropout rates, states and districts differ with respect to what counts as success and failure in the numerator. Some agencies count only regular diplomas as successes, while others also count GEDs and alternative credentials.

The second source is surveys like the National Longitudinal Surveys and the set of longitudinal surveys administered by NCES (i.e., NLS, HS&B, NELS, and ELS, all described in the previous section), which are based on surveys of samples of students. In each of its longitudinal surveys, NCES began by selecting stratified, nationally representative samples of students in the focal grade(s) in the base year. Those students were then followed periodically, allowing for the computation of individual cohort dropout and completion rates. The data sets include information about whether, when, and how students completed school. Here, the denominator of the cohort rate consists of all sampled students who were in the same grade at the same point in time. The numerator can be defined to answer the question of interest, depending on whether the desired rate is for graduates, dropouts, all completers (including GED recipients), on-time graduates, eventual graduates, and so on.

Individual cohort dropout and completion rates obtained from administrative data differ in several ways from those computed using data on samples of students (such as from NCES or elsewhere). Most importantly, rates based on administrative data are typically used to characterize dropout and completion in a particular state, district, or school. As such, the denominator must be adjusted to account for entry and exit into the population of interest, such as when students transfer into or out of a school, to other educational settings (GED or adult education programs), are incarcerated or expelled, or die.

Individual cohort dropout and completion rates that are derived from the NCES samples are typically intended to characterize large populations of students, such as all students or all African American students in the United States. Rates that are based on state administrative data provide an estimate of how well schools, districts, and states are "holding" their students and give an ultimate estimate of how many students are succeeding or failing in the jurisdiction. As such, they are more useful for determining the effects of programs and policies on students' risk of graduating or dropping out than are NCES-based rates. Unlike rates based on samples, these rates include all students, so there is less risk of sample selection bias.

The difference in purpose is partly attributable to the nature of the longitudinal cohort samples themselves. The NCES cohorts, for instance, have been conducted at roughly 10-year intervals and are not sufficiently large to characterize school districts or even states. They are thus not useful for school accountability purposes. Because student-level characteristics are publicly available in these data sets, analyses generally focus on understanding the student-level correlates of high school completion or dropping out. Researchers are also at liberty to use the data to construct cohort dropout and completion rates that suit their own purposes and that differ with respect to the technical definitions of both the numerator and the denominator. Finally, because NCES samples include students in both public and private schools, the findings generalize to all students, unlike administrative data, which are collected only for public school students. However, the validity of findings from the NCES studies is compromised to the extent that there is differential attrition of students from the samples across time. Moreover, students in the baseline sample are not representative of students in high school grades in later years because of in-migration and grade retention. Thus, in NELS88, the sample of eighth graders of 1988 was augmented in grade 12 in 1992 to make it representative of all high school seniors in that year.

Aggregate Cohort Rates

Aggregate cohort rates are designed to approximate true cohort rates (i.e., cohort rates based on individuals tracked over time) when longitudinal data are not available. Beginning with a count of the number of individuals who share a common characteristic at one point in time (e.g., students entering high school), aggregate cohort rates estimate the percentage of individuals who transition into a new status (e.g., high school completion) by a subsequent point in time. With these rates, the numerator is the number of dropouts or completers in a cohort, and the denominator is the number of students at risk of dropping out or completing.

Aggregate cohort rates are primarily based on aggregated administrative data collected from schools. All that is required is the number of students completing and/or dropping out at a point in time and the number of students at risk of doing so; this information is usually tied to specific cohorts of incoming students. No data are obtained to link observations of individual students across time.

Determining the denominator of an aggregated cohort rate can be difficult. For most purposes, the denominator should include only first-time ninth graders[9] and should account for student migration into and out of the cohort.

---

[9]In Chapter 3, we discuss the impact of including only first-time ninth graders versus students who are repeating grade 9.

However, this is difficult to do in the absence of longitudinal data. Many states have calculated an aggregated cohort rate by dividing the number of completers in the spring of a given academic year by a denominator that is the sum of the number of students who completed high school in the spring of that year plus the number of dropouts over the four prior years. Such rates have the disadvantage of including multiple counts of dropouts who entered and left high school more than once, and they fail to include as completers those dropouts from one school who later enrolled in and completed high school in another school. They also omit students whose final status cannot be determined and may therefore discourage school systems from trying to identify the final status of such students if they are typically dropouts.

Several alternative methods have been proposed for dealing with the problem in the denominator of these rates (i.e., correctly determining the number of students in the cohort). Prominent examples of alternatives, all of which use data from the State Nonfiscal Survey of the CCD, include (1) the Cumulative Promotion Index (CPI) developed by Swanson (Editorial Projects in Education, 2008; Swanson and Chaplin, 2003); (2) the Averaged Freshman Graduation Rate (AFGR) used by NCES (Seastrom et al., 2006a, 2006b); (3) the Adjusted Completion Rate (ACR) developed by Greene (Greene and Forster, 2003; Greene and Winters, 2002); and (4) the Estimated Completion Rate (ECR) developed by Warren (2005; Warren and Halpern-Manners, forthcoming).

All of these measures make some effort to adjust the denominator—which is based on the *total* number of ninth graders—to account for migration into and out of the "at risk" population and/or to account for bias introduced by the fact that some ninth graders are not first-time ninth graders.[10] For instance, the AFGR uses a "smoothed" denominator that attempts to account for higher grade retentions in grade 9 by forming an average of grade 8, 9, and 10 enrollments. Alternatively, the CPI rate is calculated by first dividing the number of regular diploma recipients in the spring of a given year by the grade 12 enrollment in the fall of that year and then multiplying this proportion by a promotion index for the three prior years. The promotion index is intended to estimate the likelihood of a "9th grader from a particular district completing high school with a regular diploma in four years given the conditions in that district during the school year" (Swanson, 2003, p. 15).

As Warren (2008) demonstrates (see footnote 10), the adjustments used for the AFGR, the CPI, and the ACR do not actually compensate for these biases. The resulting estimates of the graduation rate are in some cases upwardly biased and in some cases downwardly biased, and the extent of bias worsens when

---

[10]The adjustment procedures used by these rates are too computationally complex to explain in the body of this report. A more complete explanation of the procedures used for all four aggregate cohort rates appears in Warren (2008, pp. 30-38).

moving from rates reported at the state level to rates reported for substate levels (i.e., districts). Warren's own rate (the ECR) shows less bias than the other three at the state level, but it is also biased at the substate level, where it is subject to sampling error.

These aggregate cohort rates also have problems with the numerator. That is, they are unable to distinguish on-time graduates from other graduates—all that is known is the total number of graduates. Although these rates are frequently used to characterize the holding power of states, districts, and schools, they are conceptually imperfect for this use. Because of this limitation, they do not meet the graduation rate definition spelled out by the National Governors Association (NGA) Compact or in the most recent regulations for the No Child Left Behind (NCLB) Act and hence are not useful for accountability purposes.

Despite these weaknesses, aggregate cohort rates have one major advantage. They can be computed for every state and every local education agency in the country in a technically consistent manner, and they are available annually for many prior years. This allows for meaningful comparisons over time and across locales. The same cannot be said of true cohort rates. When based on longitudinal administrative data, true cohort rates are generally not computed in a consistent manner across locales or over time (although the NGA Compact and the NCLB regulations may change this). When based on longitudinal survey data on students, true cohort rates usually cannot be generalized to districts or even (in many cases) states. For any analyses of change in completion or dropout rates over time and/or across locales, aggregate cohort rates are all that are available.

The problems with aggregate cohort rates are important because the rates have been widely reported, have received considerable attention, and have been used to make judgments about the quality of education in specific states, districts, and schools. For instance, the AFGR is routinely reported by NCES. The CPI is routinely used for the graduation rates reported by the Editorial Projects in Education's *Diploma Counts* publications (e.g., 2008), which receive considerable publicity. The other two (ACR and ECR) have received somewhat less attention, in part because they have been used primarily for research purposes.

In addition, Balfanz and Legters (2004) describe and use a Promoting Power Index (PPI), which they argue serves as an indirect indicator of the rate at which a school system graduates students. The measure is based on the ratio of the number of enrolled twelfth graders in one year to the number of enrolled ninth graders three years earlier (or else the number of tenth graders enrolled two years earlier when school systems do not enroll ninth graders).[11] These authors, as well as other users of this measure (e.g., the Alliance for Excellent Education), are forthcoming about the potential weaknesses of this measure. For one thing, it does not actually include the number of graduates

---

[11]See http://www.all4ed.org/about_the_crisis/schools/state_and_local_info/promotingpower.

from a school system in its calculation; thus it does not account for individuals who are enrolled in grade 12 in the fall but who do not go on to graduate. For another, it does nothing to adjust for the known biases in such measures that arise as the result of grade retention or student migration.

The problems with these aggregate cohort rates lead us to the following conclusion:

CONCLUSION 4-1: Aggregate cohort indicators, such as the Averaged Freshman Graduation Rate (AFGR), the Promoting Power Index (PPI), and the Cumulative Proportion Index (CPI), are useful as rough approximations of graduation rates. However, the rates are too imprecise to be used to make fine distinctions, such as to compare graduation rates across states, districts, or schools or across time.

RECOMMENDATIONS

There is no one best measure of high school dropout or completion. Different methods of calculating graduation, completion, and dropout rates will be more or less useful for different purposes and more or less valid and reliable for different types of students. The technical issues need to be considered in the context of how the resulting statistics are to be used, knowing that they will serve different purposes. For instance, some rates are more appropriate for providing information about the human capital of the country's population, some are more appropriate for characterizing schools' holding power, and some are more appropriate for characterizing students' success at navigating through high school. Once the purpose is established, some methods are more appropriate than others. We therefore recommend:

RECOMMENDATION 4-1: The choice of a dropout or completion indicator should be based on the purpose and uses of the indicator.

We note that when dropout and graduation rates are reported in documents that are used for multiple purposes, multiple types of rates should be reported. Decisions about the types of rates to report should be based on the intended audience and uses of the information.

Our review also suggests that cohort rates based on aggregate data are not sufficiently accurate for research, policy, or accountability decisions. When these rates are used to make fine distinctions, such as to make comparisons across states, districts, or schools or across time, they may lead to erroneous conclusions. Three methods for calculating aggregate cohort rates—the Promoting Power Index, the Averaged Freshman Graduation Rate, and the Cumulative Proportion Index—are commonly used and receive wide attention. The PPI is used by the Alliance for Excellent Education and others. The AFGR is used by the National Center for Education Statistics to report district- and state-level graduation rates and, by virtue of being produced by the federal government, has an implicit stamp of legitimacy that is not justified. The CPI is used in *Diplomas Count*, the annual publication by Editorial Projects in Education that summarizes states' and districts' progress in graduating their students. Use of these rates should be phased out in favor of true cohort rates. The most accurate cohort rates are those based on individual longitudinal data. Whenever possible, longitudinal data should be used to calculate these rates. We therefore recommend:

> **RECOMMENDATION 4-2:** Whenever possible, dropout and completion rates should be based on individual student-level data. This allows for the greatest flexibility and transparency with respect to how data analysts handle important methodological issues that arise in defining the numerator and the denominator of these rates.

> **RECOMMENDATION 4-3:** The Averaged Freshman Graduation Rate, the Cumulative Proportion Index, the Promoting Power Index, and similar measures based on aggregate-level data produce demonstrably biased estimates. These indicators should be phased out in favor of true longitudinal rates, particularly to report district-level rates or to make comparisons across states, districts, and schools or over time.

If additional information were collected through the ACS, it would be possible to calculate robust individual cohort rates nationally and for individual states. The ACS already ascertains whether people complete high school via a GED or diploma, but questions could be added to determine the state and year in which people first entered ninth grade and the state and year in which they completed high school. Using this information, one could reliably estimate the percentage of first-time ninth graders who obtained high school diplomas and/or GEDs (on time or otherwise) for multiple cohorts of students. These rates could be calculated nationally and for states, although sample size restrictions in the ACS would prevent drawing conclusions at the district level. We therefore recommend:

> **RECOMMENDATION 4-4:** The U.S. Department of Education should explore the feasibility of adding several questions to the American Community Survey so the survey data can be used to estimate state graduation rates. This can be accomplished by ascertaining the year and state in which individuals first started high school, the year and state in which they exited high school, and the method of exiting high school (i.e., diploma, GED, dropping out). These additional questions could be asked about all individuals over age 16, but, in order to minimize problems associated with

recall errors and selective mortality, we suggest that these items be asked only of individuals between the ages of 16 and 45.

In the past few years, dropout and graduation rates have received much attention, in part because of discrepancies in the reported rates. These discrepancies have arisen as a result of different ways of calculating the rates, different purposes for the rates, and different ways of defining terms and populations of interest. The federal government can do much to help ameliorate the confusion about the rates. For instance, in 2008, it provided regulatory guidance about how the rates were to be calculated and reported to meet the requirements of NCLB. The National Governors Association's definition of graduation rates provides a good starting point for standardizing practice in the way that these rates are determined. However, the definition is not specific enough to ensure that rates are comparable across states. We therefore recommend:

RECOMMENDATION 4-5: The federal government should continue to promote common definitions of a broad array of dropout, graduation, and completion indicators and also to describe the appropriate uses and limitations of each statistic.

5

Early Warning Indicators

Dropping out is not something that occurs at a single point in time. A growing body of research suggests that dropping out is but the final stage in a dynamic and cumulative process of disengagement from school (Appleton et al., 2006; Finn and Cox, 1992; Glanville and Wildhagen, 2007; Klem and Connell, 2004; Rossi and Montgomery, 1994; Rumberger, 1987; forthcoming; Rumberger and Arelleno, 2007). Disengagement may begin as early as elementary school, when students fail to become involved in either the academic or the social aspects of school. Poor performance on assignments, misbehavior, failure to do homework, and lack of participation in extracurricular activities are all signs of disengagement, which often leads to frequent absences, retention in grade, and repeated transfers to other schools.

A number of research studies substantiate that these signs of disengagement are precursors to dropping out, and students may advertise their intentions fairly early on. As Robert Balfanz, a researcher with Johns Hopkins University, stated at the workshop, some students are "waving their hands wildly saying 'if you don't do something drastic, I'm not going to graduate.'" The key to reducing the dropout rate is to notice these behaviors and intervene at a stage when there is a chance for correction.

It is important to note that much of the research on this topic is descriptive. The research documents associations between certain behaviors and dropping out, but does not necessarily support conclusions that these characteristics *cause* students to drop out. It could well be that other factors are the underlying problem, and these factors cause students both to become disengaged from school and to drop out.

During the workshop, several presentations focused on research identifying the precursors of dropping out. In this chapter, we first discuss the findings from this research and then describe ways that data systems can be developed to incorporate these indicators and used to develop intervention strategies.

RESEARCH ON PRECURSORS TO DROPPING OUT

A considerable body of research exists on precursors to dropping out, but research findings are not entirely definitive, and the advice they offer has evolved over time (see, e.g., literature reviews in Gleason and Dynarski, 2002; Jerald, 2006; National Research Council, 2001). Early research suggested that certain social and family background factors were associated with an increased risk of dropping out, such as being poor, minority, from a single-parent family, or from a family with low educational attainment or low support for education (Barro and Kolstad, 1987; Eckstrom et al., 1987; Haveman, Wolfe, and Spaulding, 1991; Mare, 1980, National Center for Education Statistics, 1990, 1992; Natriello, McDill, and Pallas, 1990; Rumberger, 1995). In the 1980s, researchers began questioning the role of individual factors—in part because these variables are beyond the control of school systems—and research was designed to identify school-related factors associated with dropping out (Whelage and Rutter, 1986, cited in Jerald, 2006). This research documented that although individual demographic factors are related to dropping out, students' educational experiences are equally important. These studies showed that students who dropped out reported that they disliked school and found it boring and not relevant to their needs; had low achievement, poor grades, or academic failure; or had financial needs that required them to work full-time (ERIC Digest, 1987; Jerald, 2006; Jordan, Lara, and McPartland, 1999). Other research has identified school-related factors associated with lower dropout rates, including high schools with smaller enrollments, more supportive teachers, positive relationships among students and school staff, and a more rigorous curriculum (Croninger and Lee, 2001; Lee and Burkham, 2000; McPartland and Jordan, 2001).

The late 1980s and early 1990s brought concerted efforts to develop intervention programs designed to prevent at-risk students from dropping out. These programs were supported, in part, by federal grants from the School Dropout Demonstration Assistance Program. Federally funded evaluations of these efforts examined the effectiveness of the approaches the programs used for identifying at-risk students. These reviews found that the approaches tended to misclassify students, resulting in programs serving students who would not have dropped out and failing to serve students in most need of preventive services (Dynarski, 2000; Gleason and Dynarski, 1998, 2002). In these studies, Gleason and Dynarski reported that many of the variables used to identify at-risk students were poor predictors of dropping out, correctly identifying less than a third of dropouts.[1]

At the time, identification of at-risk students was primarily accomplished through single-point-in-time indicators, such as checklists or questionnaires that reflected performance and attitudes in the given year only. Longitudinal information that tracked students and cohorts over time was rarely available. Insights learned from this research suggested that risk factors may cumulate from year to year and that there may be benefit to measuring trends in students' status on the risk factors over time (Gleason and Dynarski, 2002). For instance, for some students, a year of poor performance may be regarded as a temporary setback that causes them to buckle down and work harder the next year. Other students may not be as resilient—one year of poor performance may lead to another, causing the student to become discouraged, to increasingly detach from school, and ultimately to drop out.

Several comprehensive studies followed that made use of longitudinal data (i.e., Allensworth and Easton, 2005; Neild, Stoner-Eby, and Furstenberg, 2001; Roderick and Camburn, 1999). These studies considered some of the same variables evaluated by Gleason and Dynarski, but the existence of data collected over time allowed for examination of the interactions among potential precursors to dropping out and students' individual levels of resiliency and persistence. Below we discuss two series of studies that grew from work with middle school students in Philadelphia and high school students in Chicago.

Identifying At-Risk Students in Middle School

Robert Balfanz and his colleagues have conducted a series of studies on early precursors of dropping out, warning signs that become apparent before students begin high school. This work began with the Philadelphia school system. At the time the study started, most of the grade 9 students in the 21 Philadelphia neighborhood high schools were over age for the grade (older than the typical ninth grade student). At some schools as many as 80 percent of the freshmen were repeating the grade for the second or third time. Students had poor attendance records in grade 8, and their achievement in mathematics and reading was below grade level.

Balfanz and colleagues followed a cohort of students for seven years, from the 1995-96 school year (when they were enrolled in grade 6) to the 2003-04 school year (one year past their expected time of graduation). The researchers

---

[1]Risk factors considered in their research were family background variables (i.e., a single-parent family, a sibling who dropped out, a mother who did not graduate); school experience variables (i.e., absenteeism, overage for grade, low grades, disciplinary problems, record of frequent transfers); personal characteristics (i.e., external locus of control, low self-esteem, student is not sure he or she will graduate); and the presence of adult responsibilities (i.e., student has a child).

sought to identify variables that were clear and useful signals of being at risk for not graduating. Aware of the findings reported by Gleason and Dynarski (2002), they set a decision rule for the variables that minimized the number of false positives—that is, variables that minimized the chance of incorrectly classifying a student as at risk of dropping out. For this study, they selected variables that identified grade 6 students with a 75 percent chance or higher of not graduating on time. The variables that met this rule were

- failing mathematics,
- failing English,
- attending grade 6 less than 80 percent of the time, and
- receiving a poor final behavior grade in a course.

Each of the individual indicators was designed to identify students with a 25 percent or less chance of graduating. For this cohort, less than 30 percent with any one of these indicators graduated by 2003-04. Collectively, the four indicators identified 59 percent of the students in the cohort who did not earn a diploma. To corroborate these findings, Balfanz and his colleagues conducted follow-up studies in Boston, Indianapolis, Mobile, Pueblo (Colorado), and Baltimore.

In all of the districts, grade 6 students who failed English or mathematics were at high risk of not graduating.[2] More recent studies in California have corroborated the relationship between course failure in middle school and the risk of dropping out. Studying the 2006 graduating class in Fresno Unified School District, Kurlaender, Reardon, and Jackson (2008) found that students who failed two or more courses in grade 7 were much less likely to graduate than students who did not fail any classes. In this study only 24 percent of the students who failed two or more classes in grade 7 graduated, whereas 71 percent of the students who did not fail any class graduated. Another study, with the Los Angeles Unified School District, found that each failed course in the middle school grades reduced the odds of graduating, with failed classes in middle school reducing the odds more than failed classes in high school (Silver, Saunders, and Zarate, 2008).

Although absenteeism was a consistent indicator across the districts studied by Balfanz, there was no common absolute attendance threshold that met the researchers' decision rule. In Boston, for instance, the attendance threshold was raised to 90 percent (missing 90 percent of grade 6) in order to meet the decision rule. The researchers hypothesized that it may be the distribution of absences that matters, not the absolute number of days missed; that is, being

---

[2]Students who earned D's in either subject were less likely to graduate than students with higher grades, but earning D's did not meet the 75 percent decision rule.

in the tail end of the district's attendance distribution may be the important predictor.

Balfanz and colleagues could not corroborate their findings with regard to behavior grades, because this indicator was limited to Philadelphia. They investigated substituting school suspensions for behavior grades, but the findings were inconclusive.

Balfanz also examined the extent to which low achievement test scores, being over age for grade, status as an English language learner (ELL), and enrollment in special education were associated with dropping out. For the most part, these variables did not add to the prediction of dropping out, once the other variables were considered (attendance, failure in English or mathematics). Further research on several of these variables appears to be warranted, however. In a study of students in Boston, the Parthenon Group (2007) found that being over age was predictive of dropping out. The study also revealed that students who were late-entrance English language learners and special education students taught in substantially separate classrooms had a 75 percent risk of not graduating.

Balfanz and colleagues also considered the grade in which the indicator (failing math, failing English, high absenteeism, poor behavior grade) first became apparent and the relationship between the number of indicators and the likelihood of graduating. The findings suggested that the earlier the indicator first appeared, the lower the students' chances of graduating. In Boston, for instance, students who first had an off-track indicator in grade 9 graduated at nearly twice the rate as students with an off-track indicator in grade 6. Furthermore, they found that the likelihood of graduating decreased as the number of indicators increased. Students who had multiple indicators had extremely poor graduation outcomes—in some districts, only a few percent of students with all four indicators graduated.

Identifying At-Risk Ninth Graders

Another series of studies focused on identifying risk factors for ninth graders. Allensworth and Easton (2005, 2007) created indicators to classify freshman as on-track or off-track in terms of following a path likely to lead to graduation. In those studies, freshmen were classified as on-track if

- the student had earned the course credits needed to be promoted to grade 10, and
- the student had no more than one failing semester grade in the core subjects of English, mathematics, science, or social studies.

In their first study, the researchers followed a cohort of students in Chicago who entered high school for the first time in 1999, who should have graduated by summer 2003 (n = 21,203). Their studies showed that ninth graders who were on-track at the end of the freshman year were 3.5 times more likely to graduate than the students who ended their freshman year off-track. Of the on-track students, 82 percent graduated from high school within four years, while only 22 percent of the off-track students graduated on time. After five years, the graduation rate was 85 percent for the on-track students and 28 percent for the off-track students. Subsequent studies found the same patterns among later cohorts of students.

Similar to Balfanz, Allensworth and Easton found that performance in coursework was more highly associated with graduation than performance on standardized achievement tests. Their findings showed that the on-track indicator was nearly eight times more predictive of graduation than grade 8 achievement test scores. In their sample, 46 percent of the entering freshmen with achievement test scores in the bottom quartile were on-track by the end of the year, and 71 percent of those on-track students with low test scores graduated on time. Furthermore, nearly 25 percent of the entering freshmen with achievement test scores in the top quartile were off-track by the end of the year, and only 38 percent of this group graduated from high school on time.

The researchers also examined the relationships between on-time graduation and background factors, including race/ethnicity, gender, economic status, parental education, and achievement in elementary school. They found that although there is a relationship between on-track rates and background characteristics, these factors do not predetermine graduation. The on-track indicator predicted on-time graduation equally well for students regardless of their background characteristics. Furthermore, background factors did not substantially improve the prediction of graduation once students' grade 9 course performance was considered.

Although the on-track variable is easy to understand and to calculate, one drawback is that it cannot be calculated until students complete the freshman year. To compensate for this shortcoming, the researchers studied indicators available earlier in the freshman year, including grade-point average (GPA), the number of semester course failures, and absences. All three variables were as predictive as on-track status, correctly predicting graduation status about 80 percent of the time. Again, once these variables were considered, background characteristics did not add to the prediction.

Of the variables studied, GPA was a slightly better predictor than a simple indicator of passing or failing a course because of its rank-ordered nature (i.e., some students pass their courses with very low grades). Students who ended their freshman year with a GPA of 2.5 or higher had graduation rates of at least 86 percent. Students with freshman year GPAs of 1.5 or lower had a much lower graduation rate: 53 percent for those with a GPA of 1.5, and 28 percent or less for those with a GPA of 1.0 or lower.

Absenteeism was slightly less predictive than GPA or the on-track indicator (since attending class is not the same as performing well), but even moderate absentee rates were predictive of being at risk for not graduating. Of the students who missed between 10 and 14 days of school in a semester, only 41 percent graduated on time. A follow-up study found that absenteeism and freshman year grades were as strongly predictive of graduation for students with disabilities as they were for students without identified disabilities (Gwynne et al., 2009). Furthermore, absences were the primary reason that dropout rates were so high among students with disabilities.

DEVELOPING DATA SYSTEMS TO IDENTIFY AT-RISK STUDENTS

The studies discussed above suggest that a number of routinely collected variables can be used to identify students at risk of dropping out. Early intervention is likely to be key to reducing dropout rates, and these findings provide guidance on ways to identify at-risk students as early as middle school. Building data systems that incorporate the necessary information can facilitate early identification and intervention.

Important Information

The research findings imply that early warning systems need to be able to capture, at a minimum, students' course grades and attendance records, beginning as early as grade 6, as well as credit hours earned for ninth graders. In addition, behavior measures and basic demographic, test score, and status variables (special education, ELL, etc.) are likely to be useful. Together, the findings suggest that data should be captured in its "rawest" form so that districts and states can conduct their own studies to determine the best predictors in their school systems. For instance, Balfanz advised recording actual course grades, not simply an indicator of course failures, because research is not entirely conclusive on the grade threshold that is predictive of dropping out. In some settings, D's may be as predictive as course failures (Rumberger and Arellano, 2007). Capturing both semester and final grades and noting whether the course is a core academic course are important, since a low semester grade in a core course can be the earliest sign of becoming off-track. Likewise, Balfanz advised that attendance data be recorded in terms of the number of days attended, not an overall percentage of days attended (without providing information on days enrolled), because the research was not conclusive about the absolute number of absences that was predictive of dropping out. At the high school level, absences should be recorded at the course level, because students may cut a particular course but not miss the entire day of school

A number of states and districts (such as Albuquerque, Dallas, Omaha, and Prince George's County, Maryland) have begun working on early indicator systems, conducting their own research to identify the variables predictive of dropping out in their jurisdictions.[3] At the workshop, Bill Smith, with the Sioux Falls School District in South Dakota, made a presentation on research that has been conducted in his district. We include this as an example of ways in which school systems can design studies to identify early risk factors, determine the variables that need to be incorporated in early indicator data systems, evaluate current policy, and inform decision making about interventions.

An Example of an Early Indicator System

In Sioux Falls, officials were aware of the findings about precursors of dropping out from research on students in Philadelphia and Chicago. Drawing from these results, district researchers designed several studies of students who dropped out of the Sioux Falls School District. The researchers identified three categories of risk factors for their students:

1. Academic: a semester grade of F in two or more classes or dismissal from an Individualized Education Plan at the middle school level.
2. Transition: moving into the district in grade 5 or later and multiple moves to schools into and/or out of the district.
3. Attendance: having more than 10 absences in a year.

The school system then worked to develop interventions for students with these risk factors and now has three kinds of programs in place. "Universal interventions" are implemented for all students. "Targeted interventions" focus on smaller group of students (10-20 percent) who may need some additional support to remain connected and successful in school. "Individualized interventions" are for those students (roughly 5 to 10 percent) who need intensive support in order to stay in school and be successful. The interventions used by the school system are displayed in Box 5-1.

Smith also recounted a story of how this research uncovered unintended negative consequences of a long-standing district policy. A portion of their research focused on the deleterious effects of absenteeism, and these studies revealed a statistically significant negative correlation between academic performance and days absent from school. Smith said that the data indicated that students establish patterns of missing school as early as grades 2 and 3. As he put it, "students begin dropping out one day at a time." Missing 10 days a year appeared to be the threshold after which academic performance steadily declined as the number of absences increased; the more absences, the more likely a student was to have a GPA below 3.0.

As part of this study, the researchers examined reasons for absences and

---

[3]The National High School Center has produced a tool for schools and districts to use to track early indicators (see Heppen and Therriault, 2009).

discovered that a school policy was actually contributing to absenteeism. At the time, school policy called for high school students with excessive absences to be reprimanded with out-of-school suspensions. Two-thirds of the out-of-school suspensions were for this reason. When they realized the unintended impact of this policy, district officials revised it. Current policy now requires students with excessive absences to spend time before and after school making up the missed assignments. (For additional details about the Sioux Falls studies, see National Forum on Education Statistics, 2009.)

RECOMMENDATIONS

Dropping out is a process that begins well before a student actually leaves school. Research has identified early warning signs of dropping out, such as poor grades, frequent absences, being over age for the grade, low achievement, and frequent transfers from school to school. Building data systems to accommodate these indicators is fundamental to developing systematic prevention efforts.

Although the precursor variables discussed in this chapter are useful in identifying at-risk students, they are not perfect predictors. Balfanz and colleagues used a high-yield rule to select precursor variables. Although this rule identified students who would almost certainly not graduate without intervention, it did not identify all nongraduates: approximately 41 percent of the eventual dropouts were not identified by any of these indicators. Thus, it is important that precursor variables be only one part of a comprehensive effort to identify at-risk students and target interventions. Multiple levels of interventions may be needed, as the example of Sioux Falls shows. Developing a variety of interventions that can be targeted to different audiences—some that are universal interventions that can be cost-effectively provided to all students and some that are triggered by certain factors (e.g., a sudden pattern of absences, receiving a low semester grade in a core course)—may be the best way for schools to focus their efforts to reduce dropout rates and increase the number of graduates.

Other factors, such as parental practices, have been less widely studied but may be amendable to interventions through, for instance, parent training programs. Similarly, some school factors, such as the demographic composition of the students in a school, have been shown to exert a powerful influence on student outcomes, but can be altered only through policies that directly address school segregation (Orfield and Lee, 2006; Rumberger and Palardy, 2005). Other school factors, such as those related to school policies and practices affecting potential dropouts, could be more directly altered through policy.

Although the studies discussed in this chapter provide a general range of the kinds of variables to be considered in these systems, there is clearly benefit to locally designed research. As Balfanz's work demonstrates, the variables (and

---

BOX 5-1
Student Engagement Action Plan: Sioux Falls School District

Academic (Semester grade of F in two or more classes/Dismissal from an Individualized Education Plan at the middle school level)

1. Student Assistance Team (SAT) referral. This group will provide options from the tiered list to support students.
2. Provide additional study time for students (learning centers, after-school tutors, etc.).
3. Assign staff member advocate to serve as a "student engagement case manager." This person will check and connect with the student daily (Elementary: classroom teacher, behavior specialist, counselor, etc. Middle school: core team teacher, success coordinator, counselor).

Transition (Move into the District in grade 5 or higher/Multiple moves to schools in and/or out of the district)

1. Assign a student mentor (Examples—WEB [Welcome Everybody] program at the middle school level, assign a student who will help acquaint the new student with the school).
2. Assign staff member advocate to serve as a "student engagement case manager." This person will check and connect with the student daily (Elementary: classroom teacher, behavior specialist, counselor, etc. Middle school: core team teacher, success coordinator, counselor).

Attendance (More than 10 absences)

1. Discuss interventions within the Attendance Committee at the school level.
2. Assign a social worker or counselor advocate.
3. Assign staff member advocate to serve as a "student engagement case manager." This person will check and connect with the student daily (Elementary: classroom teacher, behavior specialist, counselor, etc. Middle school: core team teacher, success coordinator, counselor).

The "Student Engagement Case Manager" program is modeled after the "Check and Connect" program developed at the University of Minnesota, which has had

---

levels of those variables) predictive of dropping out in one school district may not be equally predictive in another. We encourage states and local school districts to conduct studies to determine the extent to which the research findings apply to their students. We therefore recommend:

RECOMMENDATION 5-1: States and districts should build data systems that incorporate variables that are documented early indicators of students nationally recognized success in all three areas: academics, transitions, and atten-dance. The strategies used and record-keeping system developed for the program will be implemented by the student engagement case manager, as well as by the Title I, Part D Success Coordinators at Axtell Park Middle School and Whittier Middle School. It is recommended that the Behavior Facilitators in each of the elementary Title I buildings incorporates the "Check and Connect" strategies and record-keeping into the current program. All data will be kept weekly and monthly to monitor effectiveness. These data will be analyzed for program effectiveness and future staffing needs.

Committee Participation: Committee involvement included four teachers, two school counselors, a school social worker, three elementary principals, two middle school principals, four curriculum services and special services administrators, and two instructional support services administrators.

Action Initiatives:

- Train student assistance teams in the Tiered Intervention Model (universal, targeted, individualized) and the corresponding interventions.
- Pilot the "Check and Connect" program at Axtell Park Middle School and Whittier Middle School, utilizing a shared success coordinator supported through existing grant funds.
- Train staff members in recognizing the risk factor subgroups and related triggers for intervention.
- Implement the student engagement case manager intervention at elementary and middle schools utilizing existing staff.
- Evaluate the implementation of aligning elementary and middle school interventions with targeted risk factors and early indicators of school failure.

Administrative Recommendation to the School Board: Acknowledge review of the Elementary and Middle School At-Risk Intervention Committee Report.

SOURCE: Box 5-1 was reprinted with permission from Sioux Falls School District 49-5, Copyright 2008.

at risk for dropping out, such as days absent, semester and course grades, credit hours accrued, and indicators of behavior problems. They should use these variables to develop user-friendly systems for monitoring students' risk of dropping out and for supporting them based on their level of risk.

An important implication of this recommendation is that the interface for the data systems should be exceptionally user-friendly, enabling teachers and administrators to access information that will be useful to them in the course of usual educational practice.

We also note that it will be important for states and districts to evaluate the impact of any policy interventions that are implemented to determine their effectiveness and to consider any unintended consequences associated with the policies. The studies we discussed in this chapter identified precursors that were related to dropping out, but none of these variables were prefect predictors. Thus, it is important that any policy measures that are implemented achieve the appropriate balance between over-identifying students at risk and under-identifying students who might be at risk for dropping out. The problems associated with under-identifying are clear—students who need an intervention are missed. However, problems can also result from targeting students for intervention who are not in need of it, such as by over responding when a student misses a few days of school. Such a policy can be counter-productive. Careful evaluations of policies and programs can help to ensure that they are effective and appropriately target the students most in need of intervention.

6

Developing Longitudinal Data Systems

In Chapter 4, we described the various indicators that can be used to estimate dropout and graduation rates. Some indicators, such as status rates
and event rates, can be derived using cross-sectional data. Other indicators,
such as cohort rates based on individual data, require longitudinal, student-
level data. Calculating this type of cohort rate requires a data system that can
track students over time, at least from their entrance to grade 9 through the
subsequent years until they leave high school. Initially as a consequence of
the National Governors Association (NGA) Compact in 2005 (see Chapter 2)
and more recently because of new rules for complying with the No Child Left
Behind (NCLB) Act, states are now expected to be able to report individually
based cohort graduation rates.

During the workshop, participants explored issues related to the development of state longitudinal databases to support calculation of these rates,
and this chapter documents the information we obtained with regard to best
practices for creating data systems. The chapter begins with a description of the
essential elements of longitudinal data systems, particularly as they relate to calculating cohort graduation and dropout rates. At the workshop, we heard from
several state data system administrators, and this chapter provides a synopsis of
the work each has done. The chapter draws extensively from information provided by Lavan Dukes, with the Florida Department of Education. The chapter
closes with a discussion of the advice that the data administrators would offer
to states as they develop their data systems.

At the time of the workshop in October 2008, some states were well along
in the development of such data systems, and others were just beginning. We

think that states are likely to have made considerable progress in their systems over the past two years while this report was in production, in part due to requirements for competing for Race to the Top grant funding from the U.S. Department of Education. As a result, some of the specific details in this chapter may be out of date. Nevertheless, the basic components of a high-quality data system, as discussed in this chapter, are still relevant, and the recommendations we offer are still valid.

STATUS OF STATE DATA SYSTEMS

The status of longitudinal data systems across the states is uneven. While some states are just beginning, others have long had data warehouses capable of providing longitudinal data about their K-12 school systems. For instance, Delaware, Florida, Louisiana, and Texas have had systems in place since the 1980s. These data systems were developed to meet a variety of state needs and have served as the building block for currently existing longitudinal data systems. They contain information about school facilities, school personnel, school finances, instructional programs, and students. However, these data systems were not necessarily created to yield information about individual students' educational achievement and progress.

The passage of the Educational Technical Assistance Act of 2002 refocused data system design efforts on producing longitudinal systems capable of answering questions about student achievement. The Statewide Longitudinal Data System (SLDS) Grant Program, as authorized by the act, was designed to (http://nces.ed.gov/programs/slds/):

> aid state education agencies in developing and implementing longitudinal data systems. These systems are intended to enhance the ability of states to efficiently and accurately manage, analyze, and use education data, including individual student records. The data systems developed with funds from these grants should help states, districts, schools, and teachers make data-driven decisions to improve student learning, as well as facilitate research to increase student achievement and close achievement gaps.

In the first year of the program (2005-2006), grants were awarded to 13 states. Another 13 states received grants in 2006-2007, and 16 states received grants in 2007-2008. Thus, at the time of the workshop in October 2008, work on state data systems was well under way, with a total of 41 states and the District of Columbia having received SLDS grants (see http://nces.ed.gov/Programs/SLDS/index.asp).

To assist states with their data systems, the Gates Foundation developed the Data Quality Campaign (DQC).[1] Formed in 2005, the DQC is a national,

---

[1]The Bill and Melinda Gates Foundation was the founding supporter of the DQC; additional

---

BOX 6-1
10 Essential Elements of a Robust
Longitudinal Data System

1. A unique student identifier.
2. Student-level enrollment, demographic, and program participation information.
3. The ability to match individual students' test scores from year to year to measure academic growth.
4. Information on untested students.
5. A teacher identifier system with the ability to match teachers to students.
6. Student-level transcript information, including information on courses completed and grades earned.
7. Student-level college readiness test scores.
8. Student-level graduation and dropout rates.
9. The ability to match student records between the PK-12 and the postsecondary systems.
10. A state data audit system assessing data quality, validity, and reliability.

SOURCE: Reprinted with permission from the Data Quality Campaign, copyright 2007.

---

collaborative effort to encourage and support state policy makers to improve the availability and use of high-quality education data to improve student achievement. The goal of the DQC is to help states design data systems that contain the necessary information to answer research questions about the correlates of student achievement and educational progress. The DQC has worked with policy makers to define their questions and to identify the required data.

The DQC has focused its efforts on helping states build high-quality data systems that can effectively and accurately answer questions that cannot be answered with cross-sectional data. To this end, the organization has identified 10 essential elements of a robust longitudinal data system, which are shown in Box 6-1.

DQC conducts annual surveys of states to gather information about the status of their data system development. When the campaign began, no state had a data system that incorporated all of the elements. By 2008, significant progress had been made, with 4 states (Arkansas, Delaware, Florida, and Utah)[2]

---

funding is now provided by the Casey Family Program, the Lumina Foundation, and the Michael and Susan Dell Foundation for Education.

[2]As of July 2009, this increased to 6 states, adding Georgia and Louisiana to the list of states with all 10 elements in place. See http://www.dataqualitycampaign.org/ for most recent status of states' progress on implementing these elements into their data systems.

indicating that they had systems that incorporated all of these elements, and 12 states (Alabama, Georgia, Kentucky, Louisiana, Massachusetts, Mississippi, Nevada, Ohio, Tennessee, Texas, Washington, and West Virginia)[3] having data systems with at least eight of the elements.[4] It is important to note that this information is based on self-reported responses from the states and may not be entirely accurate. For instance, California reported to the DQC that it has student-level graduation and dropout data, yet the California Department of Education website reports otherwise: "Since student level data are not collected, cohort graduation rates that account for incoming and outgoing transfers cannot be calculated."[5]

Although all of these elements are important for addressing questions about students' educational progress, element 8 is fundamental for calculating cohort-based dropout and graduation rates. When the DQC began in 2005, only 40 states maintained student-level graduation and dropout data. By 2008, 50 states (of 51) had systems that included student-level graduation and dropout data. However, element 8 alone is not sufficient to calculate the NGA graduation rate (see Equation 2.1), now required for NCLB. The NGA rate requires that states have the facility to track students over time, as they enter grade 9 for the first time, as they progress from grade to grade, as they transfer to and from schools (both public and private) and to and from states, and as they leave and possibly return to school. Thus, the NGA rate requires that students be assigned a unique identifier, that their transitions be coded, and that their final exit status be recorded. According to the DQC survey, by 2008, only 18 states had the capability of producing the NGA rate. Another 27 states reported that they were on track to being able to produce the NGA rate, with 7 expected to have that capability by 2009, 10 more by 2010, 8 more by 2011, and 2 more by 2012 or later.[6] According to Nancy Smith, with the Data Quality Campaign, all 50 states and the District of Columbia can identify dropouts, and 49 can identify transfers.

The aspects of the NGA graduation rate that pose problems are identifying other kinds of school leaving and coding the final exit status. States must be able to distinguish correctly between departing students who drop out or obtain a GED and students who transfer to another school. At the time of the

---

[3]As of July 2009, this increased to 18, adding Colorado, Minnesota, Missouri, New Jersey, New Mexico, North Carolina, Oklahoma, and South Carolina to the list of states with at least eight elements in place; see http://www.dataqualitycampaign.org/ for most recent status of states' progress on implementing these elements into their data systems.

[4]These survey results reflect the status of state data systems prior to the implementation of the Race to the Top initiative.

[5]See http://data1.cde.ca.gov/dataquest/CompletionRate/CompRate1.asp?cChoice=StGradRate &cYear=2006-07&level=State.

[6]The number does not add to 51 because, at the time of the survey, some states indicated that they were not yet planning to report the NGA rate.

workshop, only 35 states could identify students who left school to enroll in a GED program, and 39 could identify students who were incarcerated.

ADDRESSING DIFFERENCES ACROSS STATE SYSTEMS

In the 1980s, schools were beginning to develop their data systems. These were typically single-purpose systems maintained in specific offices within the school system. For instance, high schools might have had automated systems for scheduling purposes. Exceptional student education and vocational education offices might have created data systems to collect the information the U.S. Department of Education required in return for the federal funding they received. But the systems differed in ways that made it impossible to merge and match data across systems. For instance, data elements were similarly named across the systems, but the definitions of the elements differed, as did the coding conventions.

At the time data system development began, much of the data was collected and maintained on paper, and as a student progressed through the school system, paper moved from one point to the other (e.g., paper transcript, paper report card). As states moved toward developing comprehensive statewide data systems, one of the overarching objectives was to facilitate more efficient and rapid exchange of information within and between levels of state education systems. States developed their systems to ease the transfer of student records, to serve as the day-to-day information provider for staff, to serve as the data source for federal reporting requirements, and to meet other state- and school-specific needs.

For the most part, states developed their data systems independently of each other. That is, there was no federal body that guided system development in a coordinated way that would produce 50 state systems with common characteristics. Thus, data systems vary greatly across states. States maintain data elements and program their systems to perform functions that meet their state-specific needs. These uses and needs differ among states.

There have been two significant efforts to attempt to reduce the variability among the states. First, as described in Chapter 1, was the NGA Compact, which laid out a common metric for calculating and reporting graduation rates, presumably to enable comparisons across states and districts. Second was a task force created by the National Forum on Education Statistics to standardize the exit codes that states use to classify students' enrollment status.

The National Forum on Education Statistics is a cooperative of state, local, and federal education agencies working to improve the quality of education data gathered for use by policy makers. The forum established the Exit Code Task Force, charged with constructing a taxonomy that could "account, at any point in time, for all students enrolled (or previously enrolled) in a particular school or district" (National Forum on Education Statistics, 2006, p. 2). The group developed six broad classifications that met two important criteria: they are mutually exclusive, and they cover every possible situation. The six broad categories are

1. still enrolled in the district,
2. transferred,
3. dropped out,
4. completed,
5. not enrolled, eligible to return, and
6. exited (neither completed nor dropped out).

For these broad categories, 23 subcategories of exit codes were identified. The task force developed these categories by examining the exit codes used in all of the states. They proposed the system of codes as a standard that could be cross-walked with state systems without losing their integrity (National Forum on Education Statistics, 2006).

Despite these efforts to standardize the way that graduates and dropouts are identified and rates estimated, differences among states data systems and state laws can still affect the estimates. Examples from three states help to illustrate these differences.

Florida[7]

Florida has had a longitudinal data system in place since 2004. Prior to that time, the PK-12, community college, and the university system sectors each had separate and independent data systems based on unit-record data. The current data system is comprehensive and covers all major data areas, including staff, students, finance, facilities, and programs. The system allows for linkages across all subsystems in the state and local education agencies. It also facilitates data exchanges across all levels of public and, in some cases, private education. The system can track students from the time they first enter school until they leave it and into the labor force and higher education. Lavan Dukes, with the Florida Department of Education, provided some examples of the capabilities of this state system.

For instance, Dukes showed that Florida's system can identify the number of grade 3 students in a given school year who are not in the same school in which they were enrolled in the prior two years. In the 2007-08 school year, the state recorded approximately 228,500 grade 3 students. Of those students, only about 128,000 were enrolled in the same public school in which they were

---

[7]This description reflects the characteristics of the system at the time of the workshop in October 2008. For further information, see http://www.fldoe.org/eias/dataweb/database_0809/appenda.pdf.

enrolled in the 2005-2006 and 2006-2007 school years. The data system allows the analyst to identify the remaining 100,500 students who changed schools at least once in the prior two years and connect them to their standardized test scores to evaluate any changes in academic performance associated with mobility. This type of analysis can be conducted for the total group of students as well as for students grouped by race/ethnicity or by economic, disability, or English language learner (ELL) status.

With its comprehensive student data collection system already in place, Florida was immediately able to calculate the rate mandated by the federal government in October 2008 (i.e., the number of students who graduate in four years with a regular high school diploma divided by the number of students who entered high school four years earlier). The state could compare its current graduation rate calculation with the U.S. Department of Education's mandated calculation for differences. This comparison required only an adjustment in which certain codes were included in the calculation, creating a smooth transition from the existing methods to the new methods.

Dukes also demonstrated the type of outcome information available for students after they left the public school system (see Box 6-2 and Box 6-3). The boxes show, for instance, that 65 percent of the 2006 graduates (see Box 6-2) were enrolled in higher education, while only 4 percent of the dropouts (see Box 6-3) were enrolled in higher education. And 3 percent or fewer of the graduates were receiving public assistance in the form of Temporary Assistance for Needy Families (TANF) or food stamps, while 17 percent of the dropouts were receiving this type of aid.

The state has worked hard to develop a set of attendance and record-keeping codes that allow it to accurately track entries, withdrawals, and re-entries and classify the outcomes for each student enrolled in the school system. As shown in Box 6-4, the state uses 12 codes for graduates, with the codes designed to be mutually exclusive. For instance, two codes are used to indicate standard diploma recipients and to distinguish between students who followed a college preparatory curriculum (WFA) and a career preparatory curriculum (WFB). Other codes distinguish between students who earned a standard diploma but took an alternate to the state graduation test (WFT) or were allowed to waive the Florida Comprehensive Assessment Test (WFW). The state has three codes for GED earners: those who pass the GED, pass the state graduation test, and receive a standard diploma (W10); those who pass the GED, pass an alternate graduation test, and earn a standard diploma (WGA); and those who pass the GED, fail the state graduation test, and receive a State of Florida diploma (WGD). A separate code is also used for students who graduate by demonstrating mastery of the Sunshine State Standards for Special Diploma (W07).

Three codes are used for students who receive a certificate of completion. Code W08 indicates students who earned the minimum number of credits but did not pass the graduation test (or an alternate) and did not achieve the

---

BOX 6-2
Outcome Findings for Florida Public High School Graduates

2005-06 PUBLIC HIGH SCHOOL GRADUATES STANDARD DIPLOMA - FALL 2006 FINDINGS

TOTAL INDIVIDUALS 112,578　　　　　TOTAL WITH OUTCOME DATA　98,085　87%

FLORIDA EMPLOYMENT DATA (4th QTR)

FOUND EMPLOYED	65,827	58%
AVERAGE EARNINGS - ALL	$2,405	
ESTIMATED FULL TIME/FULL QTR (FT/FQ)	16,561	25%
AVERAGE FT/FQ EARNINGS	$4,872	

Percent working full qtr is of those employed.
Est. Avg Full Qtr = earnings of at least $3,328 per qtr (min. wage x 13 wks. x 40 hrs.)

EARNINGS BY LEVEL*
Number of employed earning:

Less Than $6.40 per hr (Qtrly Wages less than $3,328)	49,266	75%
Wages Between $6.40 to $8.99 Inclusive (Qtrly Wages at least $3,328 but less than $4,680)	9,935	15%
Wages Between $9.00 and $10.73 (Qtrly Wages at least $4,680 but less than $5,585)	3,273	5%
Wages at Least $10.74 per hr. (Qtrly Wages at least $5,585)	3,353	5%

Levels determined by qtrly wage / 520 hrs. (40hrs. x 13 wks.)

FEDERAL EMPLOYMENT DATA

CIVILIAN EMPLOYMENT (U.S. Post Office, U.S. Civil Service)	66	0%
FOUND IN THE MILITARY	3,285	3%

FLORIDA CONTINUING EDUCATION DATA

TOTAL CONT. THEIR EDUCATION (Unduplicated)	73,405	65%
...IN DISTRICT POSTSECONDARY	1,069	1%
...IN COMMUNITY COLLEGE	41,818	57%
A.A. Program	20,226	48%
A.S. Program	2,108	5%
Adult Vocational	369	1%
Vocational College Credit	226	1%
Other	18,889	45%
...IN STATE UNIVERSITY	28,680	39%
...IN PRIVATE COLLEGE OR UNIVERSITY	4,349	6%

Students may be in multiple settings, therefore,
sum of detail may exceed total unduplicated count.

OF TOTAL CONT. ED THOSE FOUND EMPLOYED	44,150	60%

RECEIVING PUBLIC ASSISTANCE
(Temporary Assistance to Needy Families (TANF, Food Stamps)

RECEIVING TANF	160	0%
... & EMPLOYED	92	58%
RECEIVING FOOD STAMPS	3,324	3%
... & EMPLOYED	2,067	62%
RECEIVING TANF &or FOOD STAMPS	3,381	3%
... & EMPLOYED	2,090	62%

FLORIDA DEPARTMENT OF CORRECTIONS DATA

INCARCERATED	24	0%
COMMUNITY SUPERVISION	404	0%

Source: Florida Education and Training Placement Information Program　　　　Page No. 1

SOURCE: Data from http://www.fldoe.org/fetpip/. Reproduced by Lavan Dukes in *Data Reporting Infrastructure Necessary for Accurately Tracking Dropout and Graduation Rates*, presentation for the Workshop on Improved Measurement of High School Dropout and Completion Rates, 2008.

---

required GPA. Code W8A is used for students who met all the requirements for a standard diploma but did not pass the graduation test; these students are eligible to take the college placement test in order to enter a state community college. Finally, code W09 is used for special education students who met local requirements but not the state minimum requirements.

A set of codes is also used to designate and distinguish among students who drop out. The codes indicate both that the student has withdrawn from school and provide the reason for the withdrawal. For instance, certain codes identify students who withdraw to enter the adult education program (W26), for medical reasons (W18), or because they were expelled (W21).

BOX 6-3
Outcome Findings for Florida Public High School Dropouts

0706073

2005-06 PUBLIC HIGH SCHOOL DROPOUTS - FALL 2006 FINDINGS

TOTAL INDIVIDUALS 43,981			TOTAL WITH OUTCOME DATA 19,030 43%		

FLORIDA EMPLOYMENT DATA (4th QTR)			**FLORIDA CONTINUING EDUCATION DATA**		
FOUND EMPLOYED	12,172	28%	TOTAL CONT. THEIR EDUCATION (Unduplicated)	1,806	4%
AVERAGE EARNINGS - ALL	$2,267		...IN DISTRICT POSTSECONDARY	125	7%
ESTIMATED FULL TIME/FULL QTR (FT/FQ)	2,893	24%	...IN COMMUNITY COLLEGE	1,602	89%
AVERAGE FT/FQ EARNINGS	$5,283		A.A. Program	171	11%
			A.S. Program	33	2%
Percent working full qtr is of those employed.			Adult Vocational	40	2%
Est. Avg Full Qtr = earnings of at least $3,328 per qtr (min. wage x 13 wks. x 40 hrs.)			Vocational College Credit	****	****
			Other	1,351	84%
			...IN STATE UNIVERSITY	71	4%
EARNINGS BY LEVEL*			...IN PRIVATE COLLEGE OR UNIVERSITY	19	1%
Number of employed earning:			*Students may be in multiple settings, therefore, sum of detail may exceed total unduplicated count.*		
Less Than $6.40 per hr					
(Qtrly Wages less than $3,328)	9,279	76%	OF TOTAL CONT. ED. THOSE FOUND EMPLOYED	1,094	61%
Wages Between $6.40 to $8.99 Inclusive					
(Qtrly Wages at least $3,328 but less than $4,680)	1,532	13%	**RECEIVING PUBLIC ASSISTANCE**		
			(Temporary Assistance to Needy Families (TANF, Food Stamps)		
Wages Between $9.00 and $10.73					
(Qtrly Wages at least $4,680 but less than $5,585)	593	5%	RECEIVING TANF	728	2%
			... & EMPLOYED	145	20%
Wages at Least $10.74 per hr.			RECEIVING FOOD STAMPS	7,485	17%
(Qtrly Wages at least $5,585)	768	6%	... & EMPLOYED	1,866	25%
Levels determined by qtrly wage / 520 hrs. (40hrs. x 13 wks.)			RECEIVING TANF &or FOOD STAMPS	7,845	17%
			... & EMPLOYED	1,916	25%

FEDERAL EMPLOYMENT DATA			**FLORIDA DEPARTMENT OF CORRECTIONS DATA**		
CIVILIAN EMPLOYMENT	****	****	INCARCERATED	202	0%
(U.S. Post Office, U.S. Civil Service)			COMMUNITY SUPERVISION	645	1%
FOUND IN THE MILITARY	162	0%			

Source: Florida Education and Training Placement Information Program   Page No. 13

SOURCE: Data from http://www.fldoe.org/fetpip/. Reproduced by Lavan Dukes in *Data Reporting Infrastructure Necessary for Accurately Tracking Dropout and Graduation Rates*, presentation for the Workshop on Improved Measurement of High School Dropout and Completion Rates, 2008.

Indiana[8]

In Indiana, the use of individual student identifiers was illegal until 2001, and thus its work on developing a longitudinal data system with student-level data did not begin until after this time. The state has specified a method for calculating the cohort graduation rate that is articulated in state law and, as Wesley Bruce, with the Indiana Department of Education, explained at the workshop, changing the formula means that the state legislature must change the law. The

---

[8]This description reflects the characteristics of the system at the time of the workshop in October 2008.

BOX 6-4
Florida's Attendance Record-Keeping Exit Codes

APPENDIX A

ATTENDANCE RECORDKEEPING REQUIRED CODES FOR GRADE PK-12 STUDENTS

ENTRIES INTO FLORIDA PUBLIC SCHOOLS THIS SCHOOL YEAR

E01 - Any PK-12 student who was enrolled in a **public school** in this school district the previous school year.

E02 - Any PK-12 student whose last school of enrollment was a **public school** outside of this district, or in another state or territory.

E03 - Any PK-12 student whose last school of enrollment was a **private school** in any Florida school district, or another state or territory.

E04 - Any PK-12 student who is enrolling in a public school in this district after having been in **home education** in any Florida school district, or another state or territory.

E05 – Any student entering PK or KG for the first time.

E09 – Any PK-12 student who enters a Florida school from a country other than the United States or a United States Commonwealth/Territory.

REENTERING INTO FLORIDA PUBLIC SCHOOLS

R01 - Any PK-12 student who was received from another attendance reporting unit in the same school.

R02 - Any PK-12 student who was received from another school in the same district.

R03 - Any PK-12 student who unexpectedly reenters a school in the same district after withdrawing or being discharged.

WITHDRAWAL FROM FLORIDA PUBLIC SCHOOLS: GRADE PK-12 STUDENTS

* DNE - Any PK-12 student who was expected to attend a school but **did not enter** as expected for unknown reasons.

W01 - Any PK-12 student promoted, retained or transferred to another attendance reporting unit in the same school.

W02 - Any PK-12 student promoted, retained or transferred to another school in the same district.

W3A - Any PK-12 student who withdraws to attend a public school in another district in Florida.

W3B – Any PK-12 student who withdraws to attend another public school out-of-state.

W04 - Any PK-12 student who withdraws to attend a nonpublic school in- or out-of-state.

* W05 - Any student age 16 or older who leaves school voluntarily with no intention of returning.

W06 - Any student who graduated from school and met all of the requirements to receive a standard diploma.

W6A - Any student who graduated from school and met all of the requirements to receive a standard diploma, based on the 18-credit college preparatory graduation option.

W6B - Any student who graduated from school and met all of the requirements to receive a standard diploma, based on the 18-credit career preparatory graduation option.

W07 - Any student who graduated from school with a special diploma based on option one--mastery of Sunshine State Standards for Special Diploma.

W08 - Any student who received a certificate of completion.

W8A - Any student who met all of the requirements to receive a standard diploma except passing the graduation test and received a certificate of completion and is eligible to take the College Placement Test and be admitted to remedial or credit courses at a state community college as appropriate.

Revised: 7/07   **Volume I**   **Effective: 7/07**   **Page Number: A-1**

SOURCE: Data from http://www.fldoe.org/eias/dataweb/database_0708/appenda. pdf. Reproduced by Lavan Dukes in *Data Reporting Infrastructure Necessary for Accurately Tracking Dropout and Graduation Rates*, presentation for the Workshop on Improved Measurement of High School Dropout and Completion Rates, 2008.

BOX 6-4 Continued

FLORIDA DEPARTMENT OF EDUCATION
DOE INFORMATION DATA BASE REQUIREMENTS
VOLUME I: AUTOMATED STUDENT INFORMATION SYSTEM
AUTOMATED STUDENT DATA ELEMENTS

Implementation Date:
Fiscal Year 1992-93
July 1, 1992

➤ (Dropout codes are designated by an asterisk.)
APPENDIX A (Continued)
ATTENDANCE RECORDKEEPING REQUIRED CODES FOR GRADE PK-12 STUDENTS
(Continued)

WITHDRAWAL FROM FLORIDA PUBLIC SCHOOLS: GRADE PK-12 STUDENTS

W09 - Any student who received a special certificate of completion.

W10 – Any student in a GED Exit Option Model who passed the GED Tests and the graduation test and was awarded a standard diploma.

W12 - Any PK-12 student withdrawn from school due to death.

* **W13** - Any PK-12 student withdrawn from school due to court action.

* **W15** - Any PK-12 student who is withdrawn from school due to nonattendance.

* **W18** - Any PK-12 student who withdraws from school due to medical reasons.

* **W21** - Any PK-12 student who is withdrawn from school due to being expelled.

* **W22** - Any PK-12 student whose whereabouts is unknown.

* **W23** – Any PK-12 student who withdraws from school for any reason other than W01 - W22 or W24 – W27.

W24 - Any PK-12 student who withdraws from school to attend a Home Education program.

W25 - Any student under the age of 6 who withdraws from school.

W26 - Any student who withdraws from school to enter the adult education program prior to completion of graduation requirements.

W27 - Any student who graduated from school with a special diploma based on option two-mastery of employment and community competencies.

WITHDRAWAL FROM FLORIDA PUBLIC SCHOOLS: GRADE PK-12 STUDENTS

WFA – Any student who graduated from school with a standard diploma based on an 18-credit college preparatory graduation option and satisfied the graduation test requirement through an alternate assessment.

WFB – Any student who graduated from school with a standard diploma based on an 18-credit career preparatory graduation option and satisfied the graduation test requirement through an alternate assessment.

WFT - Any student who graduated from school with a standard diploma and satisfied the graduation test requirement through an alternate assessment. (For students meeting accelerated high school graduation option requirements, see WFA and WFB.)

WFW – Any student who graduated from school with a standard diploma and an FCAT waiver.

WGA – Any student in a GED Exit Option Model who passed the GED Tests, satisfied the graduation test requirement through an alternate assessment, and was awarded a standard diploma.

WGD – Any student participating in the GED Exit Option Model who passed the GED Tests, but did not pass the graduation test and was awarded a State of Florida diploma.

WPO – Any student who is withdrawn from school subsequent to receiving a W07, W08, W8A, W09, or W27 during the student's year of high school completion.

Revised: 7/07   Volume I   Effective: 7/07   Page Number: A-2

BOX 6-4 Continued

APPENDIX A (Continued)
ATTENDANCE RECORDKEEPING REQUIRED CODES FOR GRADE PK-12 STUDENTS
(Continued)

➤ **Listed below is a summary of the Dropout and Diploma Codes.**

Dropout Codes: DNE, W05, W13, W15, W18, W21, W22, W23

Diploma Codes:
Standard Diplomas: W06, W6A, W6B, W10, WFA, WFB,WFT, WFW, WGA
Certificates of Completion W08, W8A, W09
Special Diplomas:W07, W27
State of Florida Diploma: WGD

BOX 6-5
Indiana's Attendance Record-Keeping Exit Codes

01 = Record of school failure	16 = Expulsion
02 = Disinterest in curriculum	17 = Missing but located
03 = Interpersonal problems	18 = Failure of Graduation Qualifying Exam
04 = Incorrigibility	19 = Transferred
05 = Need to earn money	20 = Removed by parents
06 = Poor home environment	21 = Deceased
07 = Drug abuse	22 = Permanently incarcerated
08 = Marriage	23 = Placement by court order
09 = Pregnancy	24 = Enrollment in a virtual school
10 = Poor health	25 = Transferred out of state
11 = Friends or peer pressure	26 = Missing
12 = Armed services enlistment	27 = Foreign exchange student
13 = Court ordered	28 = Religious beliefs
14 = Unknown or no shows	29 = Special education
15 = Not applicable as of 06-07	30 = Earned GED

SOURCE: Bruce (2008).

---

law has gone through several iterations. At present, state law specifies a formula that is slightly different from the NGA formula, specifically:

[T]he department shall determine and report a statewide graduation rate that is consistent with guidelines developed by the [NGA]. If the guidelines are unclear or allow flexibility in determination, the requirements of this chapter apply to the determination of a statewide graduation rate. However, cohort members who leave after less than one (1) year of attendance in an Indiana school and whose location cannot be determined may not be subtracted in the calculation of a statewide graduation rate.

This slight change in the way that transfer students are treated in the denominator produces state rates in Indiana that differ slightly from the NGA rates. At the workshop, Bruce demonstrated the impact of these differences. For a sample cohort of 648 of which 472 were graduates, the state formula yielded a graduation rate of 76.5 percent, whereas the NGA formula yielded a rate of 75.7 percent.

To classify students' enrollment status, the state uses 30 exit codes (see Box 6-5), which are also defined by law or by state board rule.[9] Codes 1 through

---

[9]See http://www.doe.in.gov/stn/pdf/2007-DM.pdf for additional details about Indiana's coding system.

18 are used for dropouts, and codes 19 through 30 are used to designate transfers. This coding scheme creates some complexities because the codes are not mutually exclusive. For instance, codes 1 through 18 are actually reasons for dropping out. Although a student may actually have multiple reasons for leaving, only one code can be designated for a student per year. Bruce commented that, in an ideal system, one code would be used to indicate that the student dropped out and subcategories would be used to document the reason for leaving. However, changing the coding system would require a change in state law.

The state has three codes for missing students (14, 17, and 26). These cover students who were enrolled at some point but are not currently enrolled and not verified as transfers. In Indiana the original school is held responsible for these students unless their status as a transfer can be verified.

Code 28 (leaving school for religious beliefs) is a state-specific code. In Indiana, this code is primarily used for Amish students who are expected to leave school after grade 8 in order to work. The state has an agreement with the Amish bishops that Amish students may leave school after grade 8. Amish students are not considered in the dropout or graduation rates.

Massachusetts[10]

Massachusetts first began assigning unique statewide student identifiers in 2000 and had the first statewide collection of data during the 2001-02 school year. At the time, the state collected 35 elements primarily focused on the demographic information that they were required to report to the federal government. The state did not use any of the information for assessment, funding, or accountability purposes for the first two years, which allowed time to create, test, and clean the data and the system. After the first few years, they added data elements in order to include programmatic information needed to assess what was happening in schools and how to improve instruction.

Prior to 2006, the state required schools to produce a graduation rate for NCLB, as mandated by state law. However, in Massachusetts, they actually produced a rate that was the percentage of enrolled twelfth graders who passed the state exit exam—referred to as a "competency determination rate." Rob Curtin, with the Massachusetts Department of Education, pointed out that they were not able to produce the cohort rate before 2006 because the data were not available; that is, the system began in the 2001-02 school year, and it takes five years to accumulate the needed data. They now use a formula that is similar to the NGA formula, with minor adjustments. One adjustment is that the span of time is "within four years" not "in four years" in order to include the three-year graduates. The cohort is defined as first-time ninth graders,

---

[10]This description reflects the characteristics of the system at the time of the workshop in October 2008.

and they are followed through the summer of the fourth year. This practice of including summer graduates is not uniform across the country. For instance, Jeanine Hildreth, with the Baltimore City Schools, indicated that summer graduates are attributed to the next class in Maryland, and Mel Riddile, with the National Association of Secondary School Principals, said that when he was a principal, students who fulfilled graduation requirements in the summer following completion of grade 12 were treated as dropouts/nongraduates in calculating the graduation rates.

The Massachusetts policy also specifies how subgroup performance is reported. Students classified as ELL, low income, or special education are included with the subgroup for the cohort graduation rate if they were reported in the subgroup for any one of the four years of high school. The rationale behind this policy is to give districts credit for keeping those students through the four years.

Massachusetts uses a set of 21 codes to indicate students' enrollment status (see Box 6-6). The state has a series of codes to designate transfers. Code 20 indicates that the student has transferred to another public school in the state. When students are given this status, officials must scour the state records and confirm their location. Failure to locate them means they are coded as dropouts. Curtin noted that this requirement is relatively new to the system, and when it was implemented the dropout rate increased by nearly half a percent. School officials are also expected to verify out-of-state transfers by confirming that they have received a request for records from the receiving state. Curtin said that although this requirement is difficult to enforce, compliance is confirmed through state audits of local school systems.

The state maintains a GED database that permits tracking students who leave to confirm that they are enrolled in a diploma-granting adult education course. Students who obtain a GED by October 1 of the following year are removed from the state's dropout count. GED recipients are not considered graduates, however; they are treated as a distinct group from dropouts and graduates.

One difference from Indiana is that Massachusetts does not have a code for missing. Curtin indicated that if a student is reported in one data collection, they have to be tracked down and reported on in the next data collection.

Code 9 is reserved for special education students who have reached the maximum age of 21 and are released from school even though they have not received a diploma or a certificate of attainment. Those students are reported in a separate category and are not included in either dropout rates or graduation rates. They are nongraduates, but not dropouts. They are not included in the denominator for the cohort.

BOX 6-6
Massachusetts Attendance Record-Keeping Exit Codes

01 Enrolled
04 Graduate with a competency determination
05 Permanent exclusion (expulsion)
06 Deceased
09 Reached maximum age, did not graduate or receive a Certificate of Attainment
10 Certificate of Attainment
11 Completed grade 12 and district-approved program (district does not offer a Certificate of Attainment)
20 Transferred — In state public
21 Transferred — In state private
22 Transferred — Out-of-state (public or private)
23 Transferred — Home-school
24 Transferred — Adult diploma program, leading to MA diploma
30 Dropout — Enrolled in a nondiploma-granting adult education program
31 Dropout — Entered Job Corps
32 Dropout — Entered the military
33 Dropout — Incarcerated, district no longer providing educational services
34 Dropout — Left due to employment
35 Dropout — Confirmed dropout, plans unknown
36 Dropout — Student status/location unknown
40 Not enrolled but receiving special education services only
41 Transferred — No longer receiving special education services only

SOURCE: Data from http://www.doemass.org/infoservices/data/sims/enroll_validations.pdf. Reproduced by Robert Curtin in *A Long Road to a Longitudinal Data System*, presentation for the Workshop on Improved Measurement of High School Dropout and Completion Rates, 2008.

CHARACTERISTICS OF AN EFFECTIVE DATA SYSTEM

The representatives of state departments of education who participated in the workshop are in charge of some of the most comprehensive data systems in the country. These panelists offered a number of suggestions for states as they work to create their longitudinal data systems. In addition, publications available through the DQC provide advice to states about data system development (see Data Quality Campaign, 2006a, 2006b, 2006c, 2007). The suggestions drawn from these sources are discussed below.

Suggestions for States

One key issue is identifying the intended functions of the system so they can guide the development project. Given the current focus on accountability, some of the functions systems should be able to perform include:

1. Following students' academic progress and examining progress for critical subgroups, such as by race/ethnicity, gender, social/economic status, English proficiency, and disability status.
2. Determining the effectiveness of specific schools and programs.
3. Identifying high-performing schools and districts so that educators and policy makers can determine the factors that contribute to high academic performance.
4. Evaluating the effect of teacher preparation and training programs on student achievement by connecting students to test scores and teachers.
5. Evaluating the extent to which school systems are preparing students for success in rigorous high school courses, college, and challenging jobs by connecting students and their performance to higher education and workforce data.

In order to do this, comprehensive data systems need to include a variety of information about students, teachers, and the instructional programs. The workshop participants identified the following as important data elements that systems should include

- Student demographics, such as race, gender, grade level, ELL status, disability status, migrant status, and socioeconomic status (e.g., education of parents).
- Student coursework data, such as the name of courses taken, credits attempted, credits earned, overall GPA.
- Student attendance records, such as entry date, withdrawal date, days present, days absent.
- Student assessment data, such as tests taken (form, date, publication year), test results (score, performance level).
- Discipline information, such as type, context, and results.
- Teacher information, such as type of degree, years of experience, college attended, certification status, in/out-of-field status, advanced certification status (i.e., certification by the National Board for Professional Teaching Standards), highly qualified teacher status.
- Financial information capable of being linked to the school information.
- Staff/personnel information capable of being linked to school information.

The presenters made a number of suggestions regarding data elements. They emphasized that data quality begins at the local school district with the person who enters the data; accuracy depends on the quality of data that are entered. They advised states to refer to *Building the Culture of Data Quality* (National Forum on Education Statistics, 2005), which provides a number of important guidelines regarding data quality. They also advised states to develop clearly defined, carefully articulated coding systems that everyone understands. It is important to think about the codes and processes in terms of the possibilities for "gaming the system." That is, system developers should think about ways that the schools can interpret the rules other than what was intended and try to prevent these misinterpretations. To the extent possible, the system should begin with the most granular data available; that is, it is always possible to use granular data to aggregate up, but it is not possible to "aggregate down." If the goal is to compare across years, it is important that the data and algorithms remain consistent. One small change will result in inaccurate and inappropriate comparisons. Annual written documentation of processes, procedures, and results will help maintain consistency and quality over time. It is also critical to institute a process for adding elements or making changes to the data system. New data elements should be clearly defined, the coding should be understood, and the new elements should adhere to established protocol for the system.

The presenters also emphasized that it is important to take the time to get it right. Although states are under time pressure to produce the rates, it is important that the rates are not reported until the data are of sufficient quality to yield accurate estimates. They noted that there are several ways to improve the quality of data received from the schools. One way is to publicly report it. As one workshop participant commented, "accuracy always improves when someone is embarrassed by a public report." Another way is to conduct regular audits of the school systems to ensure that reporting of student enrollment status is accurate and that adequate documentation is obtained to verify the status of transfer students. In addition, extensive and ongoing staff training for the collection, storage, analysis, and use of the data at the state, district, and school levels will also help ensure data quality. Workshop participants advised that local school districts must be willing and able to comply with the requirements for creating the system and ensure high-quality data input from their end of the system.

The presenters pointed out that schools and districts will be more likely to provide quality data if they see the benefit of the information. Having the ability to access the data and make data-based decisions is key to using the data to improve instruction and educational outcomes. For instance, Robin Taylor, with the Delaware Department of Education, demonstrated how she is able to access her system on an as-needed basis to answer specific questions. In preparation for the workshop, she used her system to inquire about the annual by-grade dropout rates in her state for the 2007-08 school year. In a matter of minutes, she was able to determine that 41 percent of the students who dropped out in Delaware did so in grade 9, 32 percent in grade 10, 19 percent in grade 11, and 8 percent in grade 12.

The presenters also noted that sophisticated and complex systems are not always needed. The key is that the system be flexible, integrated, understandable, and able to grow. However, the state education agency must have the technological infrastructure, including hardware and software, to design, develop, and implement the system. The political will must exist to create and implement a system that functions with valid and useful results.

Standards for Data Systems

Lavan Dukes discussed a set of standards created by the Governmental Accounting Standards Board (GASB). Although these standards were originally developed in the context of financial information systems, their characteristics can be applied to any longitudinal data collection system:

- **Understandability.** Information should be simple but not oversimplified. Explanations and interpretations should be included when necessary.
- **Reliability.** Information should be accurate, verifiable, and free from bias. It should be comprehensive; nothing should be omitted that is necessary to represent events and conditions, nor should anything be included that would cause the information to be misleading.
- **Relevance.** There must be a close logical relationship between the information provided and the purpose for which it is needed.
- **Timeliness.** Information from the system should be available soon enough after the reported events to affect decisions.
- **Consistency.** Once a principle or a method is adopted, it should be used for all similar events and conditions. The calculations performed by all should result in the same answer.
- **Comparability.** Procedures and practices should remain the same across time and reports. If differences occur, they should be due to substantive differences in the events and conditions reported rather than arbitrarily implemented practices or procedures for data collection.

In addition, data systems that store individually identifiable information should be designed and maintained to ensure that proper privacy and confidentiality protections are implemented. There are a number of potential dilemmas posed by such data systems, and states should clearly define and implement systems to control who has access to the information, what information they have access to, and what uses can be made of the information. For instance, in addition to implementing appropriate computer security protections, the state should determine who outside of school officials should have access to the data (i.e., law enforcement officials, social services, attorneys, parents, researchers) and should define acceptable uses. Privacy and confidentiality rules are addressed in documents available from the Data Quality Campaign (i.e., see http://dataqualitycampaign.org/resources/980).

RECOMMENDATIONS

Dropout and completion rates cannot be calculated without data. The accuracy of the rates depends on the accuracy and the completeness of the data used for their calculation. State and local education agencies play the leading role in collecting the data that are used to produce cohort rates, the rates that are ultimately used for accountability purposes. In this chapter, we discussed the essential elements of a longitudinal data system identified by the Data Quality Campaign. We think that these components are critical for ensuring that data systems are able to track students accurately, calculate dropout and completion rates, monitor students' progress, identify students at risk of dropping out, and conduct research to evaluate the effectiveness of their programs. We encourage all states to incorporate these components into their systems and therefore recommend:

> **RECOMMENDATIONS 6-1:** All states should develop data systems that include the 10 essential elements identified by the Data Quality Campaign as critical for calculating the National Governors Association graduation rate. These elements include a unique student identifier, student-level information (data on their enrollments, demographics, program participation, test scores, courses taken, grades, and college readiness test scores), the ability to match students to their teachers and to the postsecondary system, the ability to calculate graduation and dropout rates, and a method for auditing the system.

States and local education agencies can take a number of steps to ensure the quality of their data systems and the data that are incorporated into them. Specifically, data systems should be developed so that the information contained in them is understandable, reliable, relevant for the intended purpose, available in a timely manner, and handled in a consistent and comparable way over time. Annual written documentation of processes, procedures, and results will help maintain consistency and quality over time. It is particularly important to maintain historical documentation of the processes, procedures, and information used to calculate the rates that are reported from the data system so that rates can be reproduced if needed and the data can be handled in a comparable way in subsequent years. It is also critical to institute a process for adding elements or making changes to the data system. Likewise, mechanisms for data retrieval should be incorporated into system designs so that usable data sets can be easily produced. New data elements should be clearly defined, the coding should be documented, and the new elements should adhere to established protocol for the system. If the goal is to make comparisons across years, it is important that the data and algorithms remain consistent. One small change in method may result in inaccurate and inappropriate comparisons. We therefore recommend:

RECOMMENDATION 6-2: All states and local education agencies should maintain written documentation of their processes, procedures, and results. The documentation should be updated annually and should include a process for adding elements or making changes to the system. When data systems or recording procedures or codes are revised, old and new systems should be used in parallel for a period of time to determine consistency.

The quality of the data begins at the point when data are collected and entered into the system. It is therefore important that training be provided for those who carry out these tasks. Extensive and ongoing staff training should cover the collection, storage, analysis, and use of the data at the state, district, and school levels. To this end, system developers should develop clearly defined, carefully articulated coding systems that all contributors to and users of the system can understand. As they do this, system developers should think about ways that those entering the data might interpret the rules in ways other than what was intended and try to prevent these misinterpretations. On this point, we recommend:

RECOMMENDATION 6-3: All states and local education agencies should implement a system of extensive and ongoing training for staff that addresses appropriate procedures for collection, storage, analysis, and use of the data at the state, district, and school levels.

An important mechanism for verifying the accuracy of data that are incorporated into the system is to conduct regular audits of the school systems. Audits can help to ensure that local education agencies are following the intended procedures that reporting of student enrollment status is accurate and that adequate documentation is obtained to verify the status of transfer students and students coded as dropouts. Audits can help to identify procedures or processes that are posing problems and can be used to improve instructions provided to school systems. We therefore recommend

RECOMMENDATION 6-4: All states and local education agencies should conduct regular audits of data systems to ensure that reporting of student enrollment status is accurate and that adequate documentation is obtained to verify the status of transfer students and students who drop out.

7

Using Comprehensive Data Systems to
Improve Public Policy and Practice

Determining policies and practices likely to improve graduation rates and lower dropout rates is no easy task. One challenge is that the problem is complex and closely related to other aspects of students' performance in school and their lives outside it. Thus, understanding and addressing the problem requires a broad, comprehensive perspective that focuses on the years both before and during high school. Furthermore, as described throughout this report, available data have sometimes portrayed contradictory pictures of the extent of the problem in this country. Enacting change and identifying possible solutions is difficult when the extent of the problem is under debate.

Another challenge is that authority for the governance of education and funding of programs is shared by the federal government, state governments, and the more than 15,000 local education agencies (LEAs) in the country. This diversification of responsibilities makes it difficult to effect widespread and meaningful changes in policy and practice, since each level of government is responsible for only certain aspects of education. However, each level of government has an important role to play, and having access to appropriate and accurate data is fundamental to performing these roles.

In this chapter we consider the types of information that can be gathered from comprehensive data systems and the ways these data can be used to improve policy and practice. Throughout the chapter, we provide examples of the ways in which such data have been used to promote effective practices. The chapter draws primarily from two workshop presentations, one by Robert Balfanz, with Johns Hopkins University, on how indicators of student performance in middle school can be used to build an early warning system that can be used to guide student- and school-level interventions; the other, by Russell Rumberger, with the University of California at Santa Barbara, on how state data systems can be used to monitor students and institutions and to modify the accountability system to help focus attention on the problem. The chapter begins with a review of the major issues that comprehensive data systems can help to inform. We then explore how the data can be used at the various government levels to improve policy and practice.

USING DATA TO ENHANCE UNDERSTANDING OF THE PROBLEM

There are four fundamental issues that more comprehensive education data systems can address. First, it is important to have useful and accurate data to compute dropout, graduation, and completion statistics, so the nature of the problem can be clearly documented. Developing comprehensive data systems that meet high-quality standards is a critical step toward improving the accuracy of data used to estimate the rates. It is also important to adopt consistent conventions in calculating the rates, so that the reported rates are meaningful, well understood, and comparable across jurisdictions and over time, and, when differences are evident, that the sources of these differences are explained. These issues have been addressed throughout this report.

Second, it is important to understand the factors that cause students to drop out. This includes individual-level factors associated with students themselves, such as their attitudes, behaviors, health, school performance, and prior experiences as well as contextual factors found in students' families, schools, and communities. Comprehensive data systems that incorporate these factors can be useful both for conducting local research to further explore the relationships between these variables and dropping out and for making use of research findings to identify at-risk students. These issues were covered in Chapter 5. The remaining two issues are discussed below.

Documenting the Outcomes Associated with Dropping Out

A third area that comprehensive data systems can help address is to further understand what happens to students when they drop out and the problems they face. As noted in Chapter 2, it is well documented that students who drop out have lower earnings, higher rates of unemployment, higher rates of crime and incarceration, higher rates of public assistance, and poorer health than high school graduates, but this information is known primarily through national survey data collected by federal agencies, such as the Census Bureau and the Bureau of Labor Statistics. Comprehensive data systems can help track dropouts after they leave high school and transition into further education and training, the labor market, and adult life and provide this information for students in a given state or school district. Although following dropouts after they leave high school can pose significant challenges, doing so can provide invaluable information. Improving understanding of the outcomes for dropouts can help to better target state and local policy.

For instance, Florida's data system can link education, employment, public assistance, and corrections data and can track graduates and dropouts after they leave the public school system. For the 2006-07 school year, the state was able to track 87 percent of the 114,172 graduates and 44 percent of the 37,820 dropouts. According to the state's annual report, 55 percent of the graduates were employed, 67 percent were continuing their education in Florida, 3 percent were receiving food stamps, and virtually none were incarcerated or under community supervision (see http://www.fldoe.org/fetpip/pubs.asp, p. 1). Although tracking dropouts is more difficult than tracking graduates, the state was able to determine that 25 percent of the dropouts were employed, 4 percent were enrolled in the education system, 19 percent were receiving food stamps, and 3 percent were incarcerated or under community supervision (p. 13). Florida's system can also track students over longer periods of time. One report documented that Florida high school graduates from the class of 1996 earned $28,252 in 2005, compared with dropouts from that class who earned $20,136 (Sellers, 2007, p. 26). Documenting what happens to dropouts after they leave school can help state and local policy makers understand the importance of enacting effective dropout prevention programs, particularly when the data reflect outcomes for local students.[1]

Research has also shown that dropping out is often a temporary status. That is, some dropouts return to school, either to earn a regular high school diploma or an alternative credential. One national study followed a group of students from the end of grade 8 in 1988 to 2000, eight years after their expected graduation in 1992 (Hurst, Kelly, and Princiotta, 2004). The authors reported that 20 percent of the students had dropped out of high school at least once. Among these students, 43 percent had completed high school by spring 1994, two years after their expected graduation (14 percent with a regular diploma and 29 percent with a GED or alternative certificate). An additional 20 percent completed high school between spring 1994 and spring 2000 (5 percent with a regular diploma and 15 percent with a GED or alternative certificate). Altogether, 63 percent of the dropouts in the study went on to earn some form of high school credential. A more recent national study reported similar results. This study tracked sophomores from 2002 through 2006, two years after their expected graduation (Rumberger and Rotermund, 2008) and found that 69

---

[1] It is worth noting here that because dropouts have had more potential work experience than graduates—many of whom continue in school after graduation—such comparisons actually understate the difference in earning power between graduates and dropouts. Because the difference in earnings between graduates and dropouts increases with age, it is important to follow students for many years when making these kinds of comparisons.

percent of the students who had dropped out had either completed high school (18 percent), earned a GED (31 percent), or were pursuing either a diploma or a GED (20 percent).

These two studies suggest that all is not lost when a student drops out. State and local longitudinal data systems can help to identify what happens to students who leave school and can study the factors associated with their decisions to return to school or to pursue a GED. This research can provide important information to guide decision making about state and local policy interventions and support, even after students leave school.

Evaluating the Impact of Policies and Programs to Reduce Dropout Rates

The final issue that comprehensive data can help address is the impact of policies and programs designed to reduce dropout rates and improve graduation rates. Research in this area is urgently needed, particularly experimental research that uses a design that allows one to make causal inferences about the effectiveness of a particular policy or program.[2] Despite the long-standing interest in the problem of school dropouts, there is relatively little rigorous evidence on the effectiveness of intervention programs.

For instance, in 2002, the U.S. Department of Education established the What Works Clearinghouse (WWC) to review scientific evidence on the effectiveness of a variety of educational interventions, including dropout prevention programs (see http://ies.ed.gov/ncee/wwc/). As of September 2008, the WWC had reviewed 84 studies of 22 dropout intervention mechanisms and found only 23 studies of 16 interventions that were scientifically rigorous enough to determine whether the intervention was effective.[3] Of those 16 interventions, 7 were effective in reducing dropout rates, 6 were effective in improving students' progress toward graduation (such as earning credits toward graduation), but only 4 programs were effective in improving high school completion rates. Moreover, none of these four programs were effective in helping students earn a regular high school diploma; instead, they helped students pass the test required for a GED certificate.

Education data systems can provide valuable information with which to evaluate the effectiveness of locally implemented dropout prevention programs, especially when they contain longitudinal data that measure changes in student outcomes over time. Such data systems can support rigorous evaluations of program impacts (Schneider et al., 2007) that can be focused at the local level. Even when a program has proven to be effective elsewhere, it is important to

---

[2]See the discussion of this issue at the beginning of Chapter 2. Also see National Research Council (2002) for a discussion of types of research designs.

[3]See http://ies.ed.gov/ncee/wwc/reports/dropout/topic/.

evaluate its impact when implemented in a particular school or district to be sure the program is effective in each setting.

ROLES AND DATA NEEDS OF DIFFERENT LEVELS OF GOVERNMENT

Each level of government has a role to play in addressing these four issues. Below we examine these roles and discuss how comprehensive data systems can be used by each level of government.

Federal Government

The federal government plays three chief roles that help to further understanding of the dropout problems in this country as follows: (1) leads efforts to collect, maintain, and analyze data; (2) issues regulatory guidance regarding calculating the rates; and (3) provides support and funding to state and local government in developing comprehensive data systems. We discuss each of these roles below.

Collecting Data

One long-standing federal role has been to collect data to support education research, and several federal agencies collect and maintain data that can be used to study dropout, graduation, and completion rates. As described in Chapter 4, this includes the U.S. Census Bureau (which collects data through the decennial census, the monthly Current Population Survey, and the annual American Community Survey), the Bureau of Labor Statistics (which collects data through the National Longitudinal Surveys),[4] and the U.S. Department of Education (which collects data through its own surveys and from state education agencies).[5] Data collected by these agencies have been the primary source for documenting the extent of the dropout problem in this country and studying the causes and impacts of dropping out. Throughout this report, we have cited statistics based on these data collection efforts.

Data collected at the federal level can also be used to support state-level research. Longitudinal data are particularly useful for identifying predictors of dropping out because the data are generally more comprehensive than those collected by generic population surveys, such as the ones conducted by the Census Bureau. One example is the Education Longitudinal Study (ELS) of 2002, a longitudinal study of a sample of sophomores that began in spring 2002, with additional data collections in 2004, 2006, and scheduled for 2010 or 2012.

---

[4]See http://www.bls.gov/nls/.
[5]See http://nces.ed.gov/surveys/SurveyGroups.asp?group=1.

This effort includes survey, test, and transcript data collected on students, with additional survey data collected from their parents, teachers, librarians, and schools.[6] This study collected information from parents on parenting practices that may be associated with dropout behavior and from students on their attitudes toward school (e.g., aspirations) and their behaviors (absenteeism, skipping school) that may be used to predict which students are more likely to graduate.[7] Although this study was not designed to provide representative population estimates for all states, data from states with large populations are sufficient to be used for research.

Using a subsample of these data, the California Dropout Research Project was able to study students in California to identify student and school factors that predicted high school graduation (Rumberger and Arellano, 2007). The study identified three student factors similar to the at-risk factors discussed in Chapter 5: being over age for grade, having a low grade-point average (GPA) in grade 9, and failing grade 9. Their analyses revealed that 44 percent of the California subsample were at risk, and only 61 percent of these students graduated from high school. Using this data set, the researchers were also able to identify alterable school and student factors predictive of graduation.

Specifically, students in a college preparatory or vocational program were twice as likely to graduate compared with students in general programs, although schools that had an overemphasis on vocational programs tended to have lower graduation rates. Two structural features of schools were associated with higher graduation rates. For students who attended year-round schools, the odds of graduating were half of those for students who attended schools on a regular academic calendar. For students who attended alternative schools, the odds of graduating were only one-fifth of those for students attending regular high schools. Thus, this research has identified specific factors associated with students' chances of graduating, although it is important to note that this was a descriptive study, not one that would permit one to conclude that these features of schools caused graduation rates to increase. However, these are factors that could potentially be altered if it was determined that doing so would improve students' chances of graduating. Future research might be designed to study the extent to which making these changes results in improved graduation rates.

NCES has just initiated a new longitudinal study of high school students, the High School Longitudinal Study of 2009 that will track a cohort of grade 9 students through high school (see http://nces.ed.gov/surveys/hsls09/). One unique feature of this study is that it will produce not only a nationally representative sample of grade 9 students but also representative samples for each

---

[6]See Overview: Purpose, retrieved January 22, 2009, from http://nces.ed.gov/surveys/els2002/.

[7]The National Educational Longitudinal Study of 1988, an earlier longitudinal study conducted by the U.S. Department of Education, has been used in more than 38 studies of dropouts (Rumberger and Lim, 2008).

of 10 states. Thus, it will be valuable for producing comparable state estimates of dropout and graduation rates for this cohort of grade 9 students.

Issuing Regulatory Guidance

The federal government also issues regulatory guidance that helps to create consistency in calculating the rates. In its role of collecting data from state education agencies, the U.S. Department of Education dictates how states compute and report education data and statistics. For instance, it requires that all states use a common definition of a dropout in the data they provide for the Common Core of Data (CCD). Specifically, a dropout is someone who

- was enrolled in school at some time during the previous school year;
- was not enrolled at the beginning of the current school year (on October 1);
- has not graduated from high school or completed a state- or district-approved education program (including special education and GED preparation); and
- does not meet any of the following exclusionary conditions:
  - transferred to another public school district, private school, or state- or district-approved education program;
  - temporary absence due to suspension or school-approved education program;
  - death.[8]

Similarly, the Department of Education has issued regulations for reporting graduation rates in order to comply with the No Child Left Behind (NCLB) Act. Beginning with the 2011-12 school year, states will be required to report high school graduation rates that, for the most part,[9] conform with the procedures advocated by the National Governors Association (NGA) Compact (see Chapter 2).[10] This kind of regulatory guidance helps to create comparability in the rates states report and the data that the federal government collects from the states.

---

[8]See Defining and Calculating Event Dropout Rates Using the CCD at http://nces.ed.gov/pubs2007/dropout05/DefiningAndCalculating.asp.

[9]As we described in Chapter 2, the NGA rate allows states to determine what constitutes a "regular" diploma. NCLB provides a definition of a regular diploma that overrides the state definition.

[10] See *A Uniform, Comparable Graduation Rate* at http://www.ed.gov/policy/elsec/reg/proposal/uniform-grad-rate.html [accessed January 2009].

Funding State Activities

Finally, the federal government provides funding to states to support certain programs and activities. As noted in Chapter 6, Title II of the Educational Technical Assistance Act of 2002 established the Statewide Longitudinal Data System (SLDS) Grant Program to help states develop their longitudinal data systems. Funding to support data system development was offered through a competitive grant program. In addition, the 2009 American Recovery and Reinvestment Act is providing funds to establish data systems at the state and local levels for improving student and teacher performance (U.S. Department of Education, 2009, p. 4).

The federal government, particularly the Department of Education, has also supported efforts to improve the quality of data collected by the states and to bring consistency to the way dropout and graduation rates are computed. As described in Chapter 6, the Department of Education created the National Forum on Education Statistics, which has organized task forces to address such issues as setting quality standards for data systems (National Forum on Education Statistics, 2005), standardizing exit codes used to indicate students' status when they leave school (National Forum on Education Statistics, 2006), and developing coding systems for attendance data that are common across states (National Forum on Education Statistics, 2009).

This kind of federal support helps states to develop comprehensive data systems, ensure that the data incorporated into the systems are of high quality, and ensure that the resulting rates will be comparable.

State Governments

States perform some of the same roles as the federal government when it comes to addressing issues related to dropout and completion statistics. That is, states collect data from the local education agencies that are used to calculate dropout and completion rates, they issue guidance to them with regard to how the data are coded and reported, and they provide support for dropout prevention programs. However, unlike the federal government, states have governance authority over public education and can directly implement policies at the school and district levels. When it becomes evident that certain schools or districts are not performing well, states have the authority to take action. For instance, the state can target specific schools for remedial programs when it becomes apparent that graduation rates are too low or dropout rates too high. Comprehensive data systems can provide an empirical basis to support this kind of decision making. There is a growing recognition among educators, policy makers, and researchers that longitudinal data systems can lead to increased accuracy in the reporting of dropout and completion rates (see National Governors Association Task Force on State High School Graduation Data, 2005; Miao and Haney, 2004; Warren, 2005; and http://dataqualitycampaign.org/survey/

actions). With more accurate rates—as well as rates that are calculated to be comparable across school systems—state policy makers can make better decisions about which schools and districts are in need of targeted interventions.

Some of the work conducted as part of the California Dropout Research Project provides an example of ways in which states can make use of comprehensive data systems. In his presentation, Russell Rumberger discussed a recent project report, *Solving California's Dropout Crisis, 2008*, that recommended that the state develop and report a set of indicators, including progress indicators on how well students in California are moving toward fulfilling the requirements of a high school diploma. One indicator might be a grade 9 to 10 promotion rate, to measure how many students earned enough credits in grade 9 to be promoted to grade 10, since research has shown that failing grade 9 courses is predictive of dropping out (see Chapter 5). Other indicators could identify at-risk students in middle school, such as those failing grade 6 English or mathematics courses or those having high rates of absenteeism. Such early indicators could be used by schools to identify students in need of support services to help them keep on track toward high school graduation. Balfanz also suggests that such data could also be used to provide additional resources to schools with high percentages of students at risk of dropping out.

Rumberger also described how a more robust state education data system could be used to initiate and evaluate intervention efforts aimed at improving dropout and graduation rates. Such systems could be used to measure the existing readiness, will, and capacity of schools and districts to better target improvement strategies, determine the amount and kinds of support needed to implement the strategies, and build capacity to sustain them. The systems could also monitor the implementation of the improvement strategies so that they can be compared with benchmarks and timelines. This might include progress indicators to provide information on the initial impact of the improvement efforts in order to identify and facilitate midcourse corrections in programs (see Rumberger, 2009).[11] Robust data systems can also help to evaluate the effectiveness and the cost-effectiveness of improvement strategies so that successful interventions can be replicated in other schools and districts (Levin, 1988; Levin, et al., 2007).

---

[11]As noted in the evaluation of one comprehensive school reform effort, "the best way to measure whether an intervention is having an effect is to measure variables more closely associated with the interventions" (Berends, Bodilly, and Kirby, 2002, p. 150). This idea was also discussed in earlier recommendations to build data systems that include "process" indicators (Porter, 1991; Shavelson et al., 1987).

Local Schools and Districts

Local schools and school districts have direct responsibility for collecting and reporting the data that states require and for implementing policies and programs that states mandate. With the help of comprehensive data systems, local school districts gain the ability to conduct their own research on dropout and completion rates, factors associated with dropping out or graduating, and the effectiveness of interventions.

The local school system is where intervention efforts happen, and education data systems can provide valuable information to improve programs and practices. In a study of district-wide school improvement in Duval County, Florida, Supovitz developed a model for a district-wide data system that serves three functions (Supovitz, 2006, Chapter 5):

1. Collecting and disseminating data on individual student performance so that teachers can make informed decisions about the most appropriate content and instructional strategies for each student;
2. Collecting data on programs and policies that can be used by district administrators to determine the types of support teachers and school leaders need; and
3. Collecting and reporting data to the public and to state and federal officials for accountability purposes.

Supovitz maintains that developing and using data provides two important benefits. It creates a sense of collective responsibility in the schools and the district, and it helps create the conditions for organizational learning, which is critical for sustaining educational improvement (p. 150).

Another model for using data to improve practice at the district level is provided by the Consortium for Chicago School Research (Roderick, Easton, and Sebring, 2009). Instead of providing simplistic answers to complex problems—the way traditional models of research attempt to influence policy and practice—this model seeks to build capacity in the district by

1. Developing key indicators for school improvement;
2. Providing support in identifying strategies for improvement; and
3. Identifying the theory of action behind new district-wide policies and examining how these policies fare in practice (pp. 23-29).

An illustration of this approach was the development of grade 9 on-track indicators that are now used to judge the performance of Chicago high schools (see Chapter 5).

A district-wide data system could help teachers and school counselors identify students at risk for dropping out and some of their particular needs, so students are provided with the appropriate support and services. The system could also help district and school leaders monitor the progress of such students and the effectiveness of the programs and services being provided, allowing them to make adjustments if students fail to improve. Finally, the system could also be used to report to the public as well as to state and federal officials the progress of such students and the effectiveness of efforts to improve their performance.

The emerging efforts to use early warning systems to support more effective interventions have several implications for policy and practice. First, the strategy of using early indicators to prevent students from reaching off-track status suggests a possible middle ground between waiting for fully operational statewide early warning systems that enable classroom-level analysis and having each school try to design its own system. States or districts could focus on establishing valid and reliable predictors for different school populations and then provide updates to schools on a regular basis (i.e., every marking period). Schools could then use simple early warning indicators (e.g., missing more than two days in a month, getting two or more office referrals, failing two quizzes) to identify students in need of additional support. The ultimate effectiveness of the approaches used by the school could then be established by tracking the extent to which the number of students reaching off-track status declines across marking periods.

A second implication is that considerable effort will need to be invested in training and supporting school personnel to use off-track indicators to develop better interventions and more effectively target them. This will include both mission building and cultural change. School personnel will need to be reoriented from thinking of their primary task as ensuring that their students meet grade-level objectives, to seeing their responsibility as keeping students on-track to high school graduation. In practical terms, the challenge is to create the conditions, supports, and rationales that promote rapid intervention after the first signs that students are in danger of falling off-track, rather than assuming or hoping that what might be seen as relatively small struggles will self-correct. Support and efforts will also have to be provided to enable teachers and administrators to take a more proactive role in evaluating the effectiveness of interventions.

Finally, states and local school districts should take the lead in integrating information from agencies that work with youth outside the school system, in particular, agencies that oversee juvenile justice, foster care, and child protection (abuse and neglect). It will be useful for both the school system and the agencies to know the extent to which students involved with the agency exhibit off-track behaviors and the extent to which they demonstrate these behaviors prior to involvement with the agency. This could lead to more integrated and effective supports for the students in need of them. It could also potentially provide the basis for the agencies to help fund and hold accountable school-based prevention efforts designed to keep students from exhibiting off-track behaviors. Philadelphia has developed such a system, known as the Kids Integrated Data System (KIDS, see http://www.gse.upenn.edu/child/projects/kids).

Balfanz noted that his work in Philadelphia with an integrated data set revealed three important findings. First, students involved with the juvenile justice, foster care, and child protection agencies, as well as young women who gave birth during high school, had very high dropout rates, ranging from 70 to 90 percent. Second, although these dropout rates were very high, agency-involved youth accounted for a relatively small portion of all dropouts. Third, two-thirds of the young men who would be incarcerated in high school and two-thirds of the young women who would give birth in high school had an off-track indicator in grade 6 (Neild and Balfanz, 2006b).

RECOMMENDATIONS

All levels of government have a vested interest in improving education data systems to help solve the problem of school dropouts, and each level can play a part. The committee makes a number of recommendations on what each level of government can do.

The federal government can do much to support the development of quality data systems. Currently, support is provided through the Statewide Longitudinal Data System Grant Program established by Title II of the Educational Technical Assistance Act of 2002 and through the 2009 American Recovery and Reinvestment Act. We applaud the federal government's efforts along these lines and therefore recommend:

RECOMMENDATION 7-1: The federal government should continue to support the development of comprehensive state education data systems that are comparable, are interoperable, and facilitate exchange of information across state boundaries to more accurately track enrollment and completion status.

Improving the graduation rates in this country requires much more than simply reporting accurate and valid rates. It requires taking actions that will improve outcomes for the nation's youth. A number of steps can be taken to improve policy and practice in this area. We first endorse states' efforts to develop comprehensive longitudinal data systems. These data systems should incorporate the information needed both to calculate rates and to improve policy and practice, such as by identifying the factors associated with dropping out, using these factors to identify at-risk students, and undertaking and evaluating interventions intended to improve outcomes for these students. The approach taken by the California Dropout Research Project provides an example of the ways that states can make use of national data sets to conduct their own research, identify precursors to dropping out, and evaluate the effectiveness of interventions. In addition to identifying individual factors associated with dropping out, this endeavor was able to identify school characteristics associated with lower dropout rates, which may be pursued in greater depth in future research. We make two recommendations with regard to the kinds of actions that states should take to improve policy and practice:

> **RECOMMENDATION 7-2:** State governments should develop more robust education data systems that can better measure student progress and institutional improvement efforts.

> **RECOMMENDATION 7-3:** State governments should support reform efforts to demonstrate how districts can develop and effectively use more comprehensive education data systems to improve dropout and graduation rates, along with improved student achievement.

Finally, we think the federal government should play an active role in this area by collecting data on the precursors of dropping out. This would allow for indicators of progress toward graduation at the national level and enable comparative studies on early indicators of dropout across states and localities. We therefore recommend:

> **RECOMMENDATION 7-4:** The federal government should collect aggregate-level indicators of student progress toward high school graduation at the federal, state, and local levels. Such aggregate-level indicators should be collected by grade level in the middle grades (6 through 8) and by year during high school (first year, second year, etc.). These indicators should include variables, such as the number of students missing 10 percent or more of school days, average number of days absent, average number of course failures, number of students failing one course or more, mean GPA, and indicators of behavior problems.

8

Summary of Recommendations

This report addresses three key aspects of dropout and completion rates: (1) the ways they are calculated, (2) the data that are used to calculate them, and (3) the uses that are made of them. In this final chapter, we revisit and summarize our recommendations in these three broad areas.

METHODS FOR CALCULATING AND REPORTING THE RATES

Dropout and completion rates are among the most basic indicators of the effectiveness of the school systems in this country. It is therefore essential that the rates be accurate and that the strengths and limitations of the rates be understood by those making use of them. In Chapter 3, we laid out five criteria for methods for computing dropout and completion rates. These methods should (1) provide the most accurate assessment possible of how many students actually complete or drop out of school, (2) not be biased in favor of certain types of schools, (3) be inclusive of all students but not double-count them, (4) be stable enough to validly track trends over time, and (5) be sensitive to real changes in student outcomes. It is important to note, however, that no indicator is perfect, and trade-offs among these criteria are almost always required. To help users draw sound conclusions about any reported rate, the strengths and weaknesses of the rate and the decisions that went into the calculations should be documented. On this issue, we make two recommendations:

RECOMMENDATION 3-1: The strengths and weaknesses of dropout and completion rates should be made explicit when the rates are reported.

RECOMMENDATION 3-2: Rates should be accompanied with documentation about the underlying decisions that were made regarding students who transfer from one school to another, are retained in grade, receive a GED or an alternative diploma, and take longer than four years to graduate.

The federal government requires states and districts to produce four-year graduation rates that include diploma recipients only. There are compelling reasons for using this statistic as the primary indicator of high school completion. Without a common definition such as this, graduation rates will not be comparable across districts, states, or time. However, there are also legitimate reasons for producing more inclusive completion indicators that allow students more time to complete high school and that include other forms of completion, such as GEDs and alternative diplomas. On this issue, we make two recommendations. We endorse the inclusion of dropout and completion indicators in accountability policy but recommend that a variety of statistics be reported, specifically:

RECOMMENDATION 2-1: Federal and state accountability policy should require schools and districts to report a number of types of dropout, graduation, and completion rates: for all students and for students grouped by race/ethnicity, gender, socioeconomic status, English language learner status, and disability status. Furthermore, accountability policy should require schools and districts to set and meet meaningful progress goals for improving their graduation and dropout rates. Rates that are used for accountability should be carefully structured and reported in ways that minimize bias resulting from student mobility and subgroup definitions.

RECOMMENDATION 3-4: In addition to the standard graduation rate that is limited to four-year recipients of regular diplomas, states and districts should produce a comprehensive completion rate that includes all forms of completion and allows students up to six years for completion. This rate should be used as a supplemental indicator to the four-year graduation rate, which should continue to be used as the primary indicator for gauging school, district, and state performance.

Because decisions about how to handle various groups of students can affect the rates, we think it is important to supplement dropout and completion indicators with information to help users accurately interpret them. For instance, schools and states have different policies for handling transfer students. Some states require transfers to be officially verified before the student can be removed from a school's roster; others have more lenient verification policies. Some schools have policies that implicitly or explicitly encourage low-performing students to transfer elsewhere. These low-performing students may be more likely to transfer to schools that have little control over their enrollments, rather than to schools that have control over which students enroll (such as charter schools). Documentation of how transfers are handled is critical for interpreting school-level rates. Also useful is an estimate of the transfer and/or leave rate and supplementary graduation and dropout rates that do not remove transfers or incorporate new students. This additional information would allow examination of the ways in which schools' policies for handling transfer students affect the reported rates.

Policies for grade retention also vary across schools, districts, states, and time. These policies, and particularly year-to-year changes in these policies, can cause trends in the rates to fluctuate over time. Age-based cohort rates can provide information to help users understand and evaluate trends in grade-based rates. Age-based rates have the advantage that they are unaffected by patterns in grade retention that may have affected one cohort differentially from another. They are also more inclusive, in that they can include students who never make it to high school and include special education students with their peers.

If the limitations associated with a reported rate are made explicit, supplemental rates can be calculated to verify any conclusions that are based on the statistics. This would require data to be available to calculate the supplemental statistics. We therefore recommend:

RECOMMENDATION 3-3: To the extent possible, data should be made available to allow supplementary rates to be calculated that compensate for the limitations in reported rates and help users to further understand the rates. Types of supplementary information include transfer rates, rates that do not remove transfer students or incorporate new students, age-based rates, and the percentage of students with unknown graduation status.

Throughout this report, we have discussed the variety of kinds of rates (e.g., status rates, event rates, cohort rates based on individual data, and cohort rates based on aggregated data) and the advantages and disadvantages of each. We have emphasized that decisions about which rate to report should be based on the intended uses. Some rates are more appropriate for providing information about the human capital of the country's population, some are more appropriate for characterizing the holding power of schools, and some are more appropriate for characterizing students' success at navigating through high school. When selecting from among the various kinds of rates, users should keep the underlying purpose in mind. We therefore recommend:

RECOMMENDATION 4-1: The choice of a dropout or completion indicator should be based on the purpose and uses of the indicator.

Our review also suggests that cohort rates based on aggregate data are not sufficiently accurate for research, policy, or accountability decisions. When these rates are used to make fine distinctions, such as to make comparisons across states, districts, or schools or across time, they may lead to erroneous conclusions. Three methods for calculating aggregate cohort rates—the Promoting Power Index (PPI), the Averaged Freshman Graduation Rate (AFGR), and the Cumulative Proportion Index (CPI)—are commonly used and receive wide attention. The PPI is used by the Alliance for Excellent Education and others. The AFGR is used by the National Center for Education Statistics to report district- and state-level graduation rates and, by virtue of being produced by the federal government, has an implicit stamp of legitimacy that is not justified. The CPI is used in *Diplomas Count*, the annual publication by Editorial Projects in Education that summarizes states' and districts' progress in graduating their students. Use of these rates should be phased out in favor of true cohort rates, which are most accurate when based on individual longitudinal data. We thus make two recommendations:

RECOMMENDATION 4-2: Whenever possible, dropout and completion rates should be based on individual student-level data. This allows for the greatest flexibility and transparency with respect to how data analysts handle important methodological issues that arise in defining the numerator and the denominator of these rates.

RECOMMENDATION 4-3: The Averaged Freshman Graduation Rate, the Cumulative Proportion Index, the Promoting Power Index, and similar measures based on aggregate-level data produce demonstrably biased estimates. These indicators should be phased out in favor of true longitudinal rates, particularly to report district-level rates or to make comparisons across states, districts, and schools or over time.

In the past few years, dropout and graduation rates have received much attention, in part because of discrepancies in the reported rates. These discrepancies have arisen as a result of different ways of calculating the rates, different purposes for the rates, and different ways of defining terms and populations of interest. The federal government can do much to help ameliorate the confusion about the rates. For instance, in 2008, it provided regulatory guidance about how the rates were to be calculated and reported to meet the requirements of the No Child Left Behind (NCLB) Act. We recognize that education falls within the purview of state governments; however, we think the federal government should continue to play a role in bringing comparability to the ways that the rates are calculated and in the development of improved indicators. On this issue we recommend:

RECOMMENDATION 4-5: The federal government should continue to promote common definitions of a broad array of dropout, graduation, and completion indicators and also to describe the appropriate uses and limitations of each statistic.

As part of the NCLB regulations, states and districts are expected to report disaggregated graduation rates, such as for students grouped by low-income eligibility, disability status, and English language learner status, and to track their progress over time. These subgroup statistics are often not comparable across schools, districts, or states due to differing methods and rates of identification and reclassification into and out of the subgroup. Furthermore, the methods by which students are placed into subgroups can lead to inaccurate judgments about educational efficacy in a school system for members of the subgroup. For English language learners (ELLs), inaccuracies are introduced because classification into the subgroup changes over time and the rate of reclassification is correlated with dropping out. For students with disabilities, underidentification of disabilities and different methods of classifying disabilities results in lack of comparability. Furthermore, because some students with disabilities are expected to remain in high school for more than four years, the subgroup statistics for students with disabilities will be disproportionately affected by decisions about the number of years allowed for graduation in the indicators (e.g., four-year versus five-year rates).

The main purpose of subgroup statistics is to gauge the degree to which schools, districts, and states are serving particular groups of students. To make these judgments fairly, alternative statistics could provide supplemental information for subgroups. With regard to graduation rates for these subgroups, we recommend:

RECOMMENDATION 3-5: To improve knowledge about graduation rates among subgroups, alternate statistics should complement conventional indicators. Alternate graduation rates for English language learners should include former ELL students as well as students currently classified in this category. Thus, records on ELL status should accompany students as they progress through grades, change ELL status, and transfer across districts. Alternative graduation rates for special education students and English language learners should allow additional years toward graduation.

DATA AND DATA SYSTEMS

Dropout and completion rates cannot be calculated without data. As we have described throughout this report, the accuracy of the rates depends on the accuracy and the completeness of the data used for their calculation. Decisions about the kinds of data to collect and how they are handled can substantially impact the rates. In the various chapters of this report, we have made recommendations about actions that should be taken at different administrative levels to ensure that the data are of highest quality. Below we group these recommendations into those intended for states and local school districts and those intended for the federal government.

State and Local Education Agencies

States play the leading role in collecting the data that are used to produce cohort rates, the rates that are ultimately used for accountability purposes. In Chapter 6, we discussed the essential elements of a longitudinal data system identified by the Data Quality Campaign (see Box 6-1). We think these components are critical for ensuring that data systems are able to track students accurately, calculate dropout and completion rates, monitor students' progress, identify students at risk of dropping out, and conduct research to evaluate the effectiveness of their programs. We encourage all states to incorporate these components into their systems and therefore recommend:

> **RECOMMENDATIONS 6-1:** All states should develop data systems that include the 10 essential elements identified by the Data Quality Campaign as critical for calculating the National Governors Association graduation rate. These elements include a unique student identifier, student-level information (data on their enrollments, demographics, program participation, test scores, courses taken, grades, and college readiness test scores), the ability to match students to their teachers and to the postsecondary system, the ability to calculate graduation and dropout rates, and a method for auditing the system.

State and local education agencies can take a number of steps to ensure the quality of their data systems and the data that are incorporated into them. Specifically, data systems should be developed so that the information contained in them is understandable, reliable, relevant for the intended purpose, available in a timely manner, and handled in a consistent and comparable way over time. Annual written documentation of processes, procedures, and results will help maintain consistency and quality over time. It is also critical to institute a process for adding elements or making changes to the data system. Likewise, mechanisms for data retrieval should be incorporated into system designs so that usable data sets can be easily produced. New data elements should be clearly defined, the coding should be documented, and the new elements should adhere to established protocol for the system. If the goal is to make comparisons across years, it is important that the data and algorithms remain consistent. One small change in method may result in inaccurate and inappropriate comparisons. We thus recommend:

RECOMMENDATION 6-2: All states and local education agencies should maintain written documentation of their processes, procedures, and results. The documentation should be updated annually and should include a process for adding elements or making changes to the system. When data systems or recording procedures or codes are revised, old and new systems should be used in parallel for a period of time to determine consistency.

The quality of the data begins at the point when data are collected and entered into the system. It is therefore important that training be provided for those who carry out these tasks. Extensive and ongoing staff training should cover the collection, storage, analysis, and use of the data at the state, district, and school levels. To this end, system developers should develop clearly defined, carefully articulated coding systems that all contributors to and users of the system can understand. As they do this, system developers should think about ways that those entering the data might interpret the rules in ways other than what was intended and try to prevent these misinterpretations. On this point, we recommend:

RECOMMENDATION 6-3: All states and local education agencies should implement a system of extensive and ongoing training for staff that addresses appropriate procedures for collection, storage, analysis, and use of the data at the state, district, and school levels.

An important mechanism for verifying the accuracy of data that are incorporated into the system is to conduct regular audits of the school systems. Audits can help to ensure that local education agencies are following the intended procedures, that reporting of student enrollment status is accurate, and that adequate documentation is obtained to verify the status of transfer students and students coded as dropouts. Audits can help to identify procedures or processes that are posing problems and can be used to improve instructions provided to school systems. We therefore recommend:

RECOMMENDATION 6-4: All states and local education agencies should conduct regular audits of data systems to ensure that reporting of student enrollment status is accurate and that adequate documentation is obtained to verify the status of transfer students and students who drop out.

Federal Government

The federal government can also do much to support the development of quality data systems. Currently, support is provided through the Statewide Longitudinal Data System Grant Program established by Title II of the Educational Technical Assistance Act of 2002 and through the 2009 American Recovery and

Reinvestment Act. We applaud the federal government's efforts along these lines and therefore recommend:

> **RECOMMENDATION 7-1:** The federal government should continue to support the development of comprehensive state education data systems that are comparable, are interoperable, and facilitate exchange of information across state boundaries to more accurately track enrollment and completion status.

The federal government can also play a role in collecting data that can be used to validate state estimates of graduation rates. If additional information were collected through the American Community Survey (ACS), it would be possible to calculate robust individual cohort rates nationally and for individual states. The ACS already ascertains whether people complete high school via a GED or diploma, but questions could be added to determine the state and year in which people first entered grade 9 and the state and year in which they completed high school. Using this information, one could reliably estimate the percentage of first-time ninth graders who obtained high school diplomas and/ or GED credentials (on time or otherwise) for multiple cohorts of students. These rates could be calculated nationally and for states, although sample size restrictions in the ACS would prevent drawing conclusions at the district level. We therefore recommend:

> **RECOMMENDATION 4-4:** The U.S. Department of Education should explore the feasibility of adding several questions to the American Community Survey so the survey data can be used to estimate state graduation rates. This can be accomplished by ascertaining the year and state in which individuals first started high school, the year and state in which they exited high school, and the method of exiting high school (i.e., diploma, GED, dropping out). These additional questions could be asked about all individuals over age 16, but, in order to minimize problems associated with recall errors and selective mortality, we suggest that these items be asked only of individuals between the ages of 16 and 45.

USING COMPREHENSIVE DATA SYSTEMS TO IMPROVE POLICY AND PRACTICE

Improving the graduation rates in this country requires much more than simply reporting accurate and valid rates. It requires taking actions that will improve outcomes for this nation's youth. A number of steps can be taken to improve policy and practice in this area. We first endorse states' efforts to develop comprehensive longitudinal data systems. These data systems should incorporate the information needed both to calculate rates and to improve policy and practice, such as by identifying the factors associated with dropping out, using these factors to identify at-risk students, and undertaking and evaluating interventions intended to improve outcomes for these students. The approach taken by the California Dropout Research Project provides an example of the ways that states can make use of national data sets to conduct their own research, identify precursors to dropping out, and evaluate the effectiveness of interventions. In addition to identifying individual factors associated with dropping out, this endeavor identified school characteristics associated with lower dropout rates, such as college preparatory programs and vocational education programs. We make two recommendations with regard to the kinds of actions that states should take to improve policy and practice:

> **RECOMMENDATION 7-2:** State governments should develop more robust education data systems that can better measure student progress and institutional improvement efforts.

> **RECOMMENDATION 7-3:** State governments should support reform efforts to demonstrate how districts can develop and effectively use more comprehensive education data systems to improve dropout and graduation rates along with improved student achievement.

To truly help improve outcomes for students, data systems need to incorporate the information needed to enable early identification of at-risk students. The research discussed in this report suggests that indicators such as the following are associated with dropping out: frequent absences, failing grades in reading or mathematics, poor behavior, being over age for grade, having a low grade-point average (GPA) in grade 9, failing grade 9, or having a record of frequent transfers. Moreover, the research shows that some of these factors may become evident as early as grade 6. Although this research provides an important foundation for states, districts, and schools to build on, the findings also suggest that the predictive value of these factors varies across school systems. Thus, we think it is important for states and districts to conduct their own studies to determine the factors associated with dropping out from their school systems. Once they are determined, measures of these factors should be incorporated into the data system so that at-risk students can be identified in time to intervene. We make the following recommendation for specific steps that states and districts should take.

> **RECOMMENDATION 5-1:** States and districts should build data systems that incorporate variables that are documented early indicators of students at risk for dropping out, such as days absent, semester and course grades, credit hours accrued, and indicators of behavior problems. They should use these variables to develop user-friendly systems for monitoring students'

risk of dropping out and for supporting them based on their level of risk.

An important implication of this recommendation is that the interface for the data systems should be exceptionally user-friendly, enabling teachers and administrators to access information that will be useful to them in the course of usual educational practice.

Finally, we think the federal government should play an active role in this area by collecting data on the precursors of dropping out. This would allow for indicators of progress toward graduation at the national level and enable comparative studies on early indicators of dropout across states and localities. We therefore recommend:

RECOMMENDATION 7-4: The federal government should collect aggregate-level indicators of student progress toward high school graduation at the federal, state, and local levels. Such aggregate-level indicators should be collected by grade level in the middle grades (6 through 8) and by year during high school (first year, second year, etc.). These indicators should include variables such as the number of students missing 10 percent or more of school days, average number of days absent, average number of course failures, number of students failing one course or more, mean GPA, and indicators of behavior problems.

References and Bibliography

Abedi, J., and Dietal, R. (2004). *Challenges in the No Child Left Behind Act for English language learners.* CRESST Policy Brief 7. Los Angeles: National Center for Research on Evaluation, Standards, and Student Testing.

Abrams L., and Haney, W. (2004). Accountability and the grade 9 to 10 translation: The impact on attrition and retention rates. In G. Orfield (Ed.), *Dropouts in America: Confronting the graduation rate crisis* (pp. 181-205). Cambridge, MA: Harvard Educational Publishing Group.

Achieve, Inc. (2008). *Closing the expectations gap: An annual 50-state progress report on the alignment of high school policies with the demands of college and careers.* Washington, DC: Author. Available: http://www.achieve.org/files/50-state-2009.pdf.

Alexander, K.L., Entwisle, D.R., and Dauber, S.L. (2003). *On the success of failure: A reassessment of the effects of retention in the primary grades, 2nd ed.* Cambridge, Eng.: Cambridge University Press. Available: http://catdir.loc.gov/catdir/samples/cam033/2002020180.pdf.

Allensworth, E.M. (1997). Earnings mobility of first and "1.5" generation Mexican-origin women and men: A comparison with U.S.-born Mexican Americans and non-Hispanic whites. *International Migration Review, 31*(2), 386-410.

Allensworth, E.M. (2005a). *Graduation and dropout trends in Chicago: A look at cohorts of students from 1991 through 2004.* Chicago: Consortium on Chicago School Research. Available: http://www.consortium-chicago.org/publications/p75.html.

Allensworth, E.M. (2005b). Dropout rates after high-stakes testimony in elementary school: A study of the contradictory effects of Chicago's efforts to end social promotion. *Educational Evaluation and Policy Analysis, 27*(4), 341-364.

Allensworth, E. (2008). *Technical issues underlying dropout and completion indicators.* Paper prepared for the workshop of the Committee on Improved Measurement of High School Dropout and Completion Rates: Expert Guidance on Next Steps for Research and Policy, National Research Council, Washington, DC, October 23-24. Available: http://www7.nationalacademies.org/bota/High_School_Dropouts_Workshop_Agenda.html.

Allensworth, E.M., and Easton, J.Q. (2005). *The on-track indicator as a predictor of high school graduation.* Chicago: Consortium on Chicago School Research.

Allensworth, E.M., and Easton, J.O. (2007). *What matters for staying on-track and graduating in Chicago public high schools.* Chicago: Consortium on Chicago School Research. Available: http://www.all4ed.org/files/Allensworth.pdf.

Alliance for Excellent Education. (2010). *High schools in the United States: How does your local high school measure up?* Available: http://www.all4ed.org/about_the_crisis/schools/state_and_local_info/promotingpower [accessed July 2010].

Amos, J. (2008). *Dropouts, diplomas, and dollars: U.S. high schools and the nation's economy.* Washington, DC: Alliance for Excellent Education.

Annie E. Casey Foundation. (2008). *Kids count data center.* Available: http://datacenter.kidscount.org/.

Annie E. Casey Foundation. (2009). *Kids count data center.* Available: http://datacenter.kidscount.org/.

Appleton, J., Christenson, S., Kim, D., and Reschley, A. (2006). Measuring cognitive and psychological engagement: Validation of the Student Engagement Instrument. *Journal of School Psychology, 44*(5), 427-445.

Balfanz, R. (2008). *Early warning and intervention systems: Promise and challenges for policy and practice.* Paper prepared for the workshop of the Committee on Improved Measurement of High School Dropout and Completion Rates: Expert Guidance on Next Steps for Research and Policy, National Research Council, Washington, DC, October 23-24. Available: http://www7.nationalacademies.org/bota/High_School_Dropouts_Workshop_Agenda.html.

Balfanz, R., and Legters, N. (2004). *Locating the dropout crisis: Which high schools produce the nation's dropouts? Where are they located? Who attends them?* Baltimore: Center for Social Organization of Schools, Johns Hopkins University.

Barro, S.M., and Kolstad, A. (1987). *Who drops out of high school? Findings from high school and beyond.* Washington, DC: U.S. Government Printing Office.

Bartels, L.M. (2008). Unequal democracy: The political economy of the new gilded age. Princeton, NJ: Princeton University Press. Available: http://pacefunders.org/publications/NCBY.pdf.

Belfield, C., and Levin, H. (Eds.) (2007). *The price we pay: Economic and social consequences of inadequate education.* Washington, DC: Brookings Institution.

Berends, M., Bodilly, S.J., and Kirby, S.N. (2002). *Facing the challenges of whole-school reform: New American schools after a decade.* Santa Monica, CA: RAND.

Bill and Melinda Gates Foundation. (2005). *Data Quality Campaign: Using data to improve student achievement.* Available: http://www.dataqualitycampaign.org/.

Boesel, D., Alsalam, N., and Smith, T.M. (1998). *Executive summary: Educational and labor market performance of GED recipients.* NLE 98-2023a2. Washington, DC: National Library of Education.

Bruce, W. (2008). *Accounting for every student: Graduation rates in Indiana. A Hoosier horror study.* Presentation prepared for the Committee on Improved Measurement of High School Dropout and Completion Rates: Expert Guidance on Next Steps for Research and Policy, National Research Council, Washington, DC, October 23-24. Available: http://www7.nationalacademies.org/bota/High_School_Dropouts_Workshop_Agenda.html.

Bureau of Labor Statistics. (2008). *National Longitudinal Surveys.* Available: http://www.bls.gov/nls/home.htm.

California Department of Education. (2008). *Statewide graduation rates.* Available: http://data1.cde.ca.gov/dataquest/CompletionRate/CompRate1.asp?cChoice=StGradRate&cYear=2006-07&level=State.

Cameron, S.V., and Heckman, J.J. (1993). The nonequivalence of high school equivalents. *Journal of Labor Economics 11*(1), pt. 1, 1-27.

Cataldi, E.F., Laird, J., and KewalRamani, A. (2009). *High school dropout and completion rates in the United States: 2007.* NCES 2009-064. Washington, DC: U.S. Department of Education, National Center for Education Statistics. Available: http://nces.ed.gov/pubsearch/pubsinfo.asp?pubid=2009064.

Centers for Disease Control and Prevention. (2007). *National Health Interview Survey 2006.* Atlanta: Author.

Centers for Disease Control and Prevention. (2008). *National Health Interview Survey 2007.* Atlanta: Author.

Chaplin, D. (2002). Tassels on the cheap. *Education Next, 2,* 24-29.

Chaplin, D., and Klasik, D. (2006). *Gender gaps in college and high school graduation by race, combining public and private schools.* Available: http://www.uark.edu/ua/der/EWPA/Research/Accountability/1790.html.

Coalition for Juvenile Justice. (2001). *Abandoned in the back row: New lessons in education and delinquency prevention.* Washington, DC: Author.

Croninger, R.G., and Lee, V.E. (2001). Social capital and dropping out of high school: Benefits to at-risk students of teachers' support and guidance. *Teachers College Record, 103,* 548-581.

Currie, J. (2009). Healthy, wealthy, and wise: Socioeconomic status, poor health in childhood, and human capital development. *Journal of Economic Literature, 47*(1), 87-122.

Curtin, R. (2008). *A long road to a longitudinal data system.* Presentation prepared for the workshop of the Committee on Improved Measurement of High School Dropout and Completion Rates: Expert Guidance on Next Steps for Research and Policy, National Research Council, Washington, DC, October 23-24. Available: http://www7.nationalacademies.org/bota/High_School_Dropouts_Workshop_Agenda.html.

Curtin, T., Ingels, S., Wu, S., and Heuer, R. (2002). *User's manual: NELS: 88 base-year to fourth follow-up: Student component data file.* NCES 2002323. Washington, DC: U.S. Department of Education, National Center for Education Statistics. Available: http://nces.ed.gov/pubs2002/2002323_app.pdf.

Cutler, D., and Lleras-Muney, A. (2006). Education and health: Evaluating theories and evidence. In R.F. Schoeni, J.S. House, G.A. Kaplan, and H. Pollack (Eds.), *Making Americans healthier: Social and economic policy as health policy.* New York: Russell Sage Foundation.

Data Quality Campaign. (2006a). *Creating longitudinal data systems: Lessons learned by leading states.* Washington, DC: Author.

Data Quality Campaign. (2006b), *Creating a longitudinal data system: Using data to improve student achievement.* Washington, DC: Author.

Data Quality Campaign. (2006c). *Measuring what matters: Creating a longitudinal data system to improve student achievement.* Washington, DC: Author.

Data Quality Campaign. (2007). *Every student counted: Using data to improve student achievement.* Washington, DC: Author.

Day, J.C., and Newburger, E.C. (2002). *The big payoff: Educational attainment and synthetic estimates of work-life earnings.* Washington, DC: U.S. Census Bureau.

Dynarski, M. (2000). *How can we help? What we have learned from federal dropout-prevention programs.* Paper presented at the Workshop on School Completion in Standards-Based Reform: Facts and Strategies, National Research Council, Washington, DC.

Eckstrom, R.B., Goertz, M., Pollack, J., and Rock, D. (1987). Who drops out of high school and why? Findings from a national study. In G. Natriello (Ed.), *School dropouts: Patterns and policies* (pp. 52-69). New York: Teachers College Press.

Editorial Projects in Education. (2008). Diplomas count 2008: School to college: Can state P-16 councils ease the transition? *Education Week, 27* (Special Issue, 40), June 5.

Education Trust. (2003*). Telling the whole truth (or not) about high school graduation: New state data.* Washington, DC: Author.

Education Week. (2009, June 11). Diplomas count, 2009: Broader horizons—the challenge of college readiness for all students. *Education Week, 28*(34).

ERIC Digest. (1987). *The dropout's perspective on leaving school. Highlights: An ERIC/CAPS Digest.* ED 291015. Available: http://www.ed.gov/databases/ERIC_Digests/ed291015.html.

Farrington, D.P. (2003). Assessing systematic evidence in crime and justice: Methodological concerns and empirical outcomes. *Annals of the American Academy of Political and Social Science, 587.*

Finn, J., and Cox, D. (1992). Participation and withdrawal among fourth-grade pupils. *American Educational Research Journal, 29,* 141-162.

Florida Department of Education. (2005). *Florida education & training placement information program: Publications.* Available: http://www.fldoe.org/fetpip/pubs.asp.

Florida Department of Education. (2008). *Florida Department of Education: DOE information database requirements.* Available: http://www.fldoe.org/eias/dataweb/database_0809/appenda.pdf.

General Education Development Testing Service (2009). *2008 GED testing program statistical report.* Washington, DC: Author. Available: http://www.acenet.edu/Content/NavigationMenu/ged/pubs/GEDTS_Pubs.htm.

Gladwell, M. (2005). The moral hazard myth: The bad idea behind our failed health care system. *New Yorker, 81,* 44-49.

Glanville, J., and Wildhagen, T. (2007). The measurement of school engagement: Assessing dimensionality and measurement invariance across race and ethnicity. *Educational and Psychological Measurement, 67*(6), 1019-1041.

Gleason, P., and Dynarski, M. (1998). *Do we know whom to serve? Issues in using risk factors to identify dropouts.* Report submitted to the U.S. Department of Education. Princeton, NJ: Mathematica Policy Research. Available: http://www.mathematica-mpr.com/publications/PDFs/dod-risk.pdf.

Gleason, P., and Dynarski, M. (2002). Do we know whom to serve? Issues in using risk factors to identify dropouts. *Journal of Education for Students Placed at Risk, 7,* 25-41.

Goesling, B. (2005). *The rising significance of education for health.* Report prepared for the annual meeting of the Population Association of America, Philadelphia.

Greene, J.P. (2001). *High school graduation rates in the United States.* The Manhattan Institute and the Black Alliance for Educational Options. Available: http://www.flace.org/MI-2001-Graduation-Rate-Study.pdf.

Greene, J.P. (2002). *High school graduation rates in Washington State.* The Manhattan Institute. Available: http://www.manhattan-institute.org/html/cr_27.htm.

Greene, J., and Forster, G. (2003). *Public high school graduation and college readiness rates in the United States.* New York: Center for Civic Innovation, Manhattan Institute. Available: http://www3.northern.edu/rc/pages/Reading_Clinic/highschool_graduation.pdf.

Greene, J.P., and Winters, M.A. (2002). Public school graduation rates in the United States, Civic Report 31. *The Manhattan Institute for Policy Research.* Available: http://www.manhattan-institute.org/html/cr_31.htm.

Greene, J.P., and Winters, M.A. (2005). *Public high school graduation and college-readiness rates: 1991-2002.* New York: Manhattan Institute.

Greene, J.P. Winters, M.A., and Swanson, C.B. (2006). Missing the mark on graduation rates: A response to "the exaggerated dropout crisis." *Education Week, 42,* 39.

Gutiérrez, A.S. (2008). *Improving measurement of graduation and dropout rates for black and Latino students.* Presentation prepared for the workshop of the Committee on Improved Measurement of High School Dropout and Completion Rates: Expert Guidance on Next Steps for Research and Policy, National Research Council, Washington, DC, October 23-24. Available: http://www7.nationalacademies.org/bota/High_School_Dropouts_Workshop_Agenda.html.

Gwynne, J., Lesnick, J., Hart, H.M., and Allensworth, E.M. (2009). *What matters for staying on-track and graduating in Chicago public schools: A focus on students with disabilities.* Paper presented at the Consortium on Chicago School Research, Chicago. Available: http://eric.ed.gov/PDFS/ED507419.pdf.

Hakuta, K., Butler, G.Y., and Witt, D. (2000). *How long does it take learners to attain English proficiency?* Santa Barbara, CA: Linguistic Minority Research Institute, University of California.

Harlow, C.W. (2003). *Education and correctional populations.* Bureau of Justice Statistics Special Report. Washington, DC: U.S. Department of Justice. Available: http://www.policyalmanac. org/crime/archive/education_prisons.pdf.

Hartzell, G., McKay, J., and Frymier, J. (1992). *Calculating dropout rates locally and nationally with the holding power index.* ERIC Document Reproduction Service No. ED 343953.

Hauser, R.M. (1997). Indicators of high school completion and dropout. In R.M. Hauser, B.V. Brown, and W.R. Prosser (Eds.), *Indicators of children's well-being* (pp. 152-184). New York: Russell Sage Foundation.

Hauser, R.M., Simmons, S.J., and Pager, D.I. (2004). High school dropout, race-ethnicity, and social background from the 1970s to the 1990s. In G. Orfield (Ed.), *Dropouts in America: Confronting the graduation rate crisis* (pp. 85-106). Cambridge, MA: Harvard Educational Publishing Group.

Haveman, R., Wolfe, B., and Spaulding, J. (1991). Childhood events and circumstances influencing high school completion. *Demography, 28*(1), 133-157.

Heckman, J.J., and Cameron, S. (1993). The nonequivalence of high school equivalents. *Journal of Labor Economics*, 11, 1-47.

Heckman, J.J., and LaFontaine, P. (2008). *The declining American high school graduation rate: Evidence sources and consequences.* Centre for Economic Policy Research for VoxEU. Available: http://www.voxeu.org/index.php?q=node/930#%23.

Heckman, J.J., and LaFontaine, P.A. (2010). The American high school graduation rate: Trends and levels. *The Review of Economics and Statistics, 92*, 244-262.

Heckman, J.J., and LaFontaine, P.A. (forthcoming). *The GED and the problem of noncognitive skills in America.* Chicago: University of Chicago Press.

Heckman, J.J., and Rubinstein, Y. (2001). The importance of noncognitive skills: Lessons from the GED testing program. *American Economic Review, 91*(2), 145-149.

Heckman, J.J., Stixrud, J., and Urzua, S. (2006). The effects of cognitive and noncognitive abilities on labor market outcomes and social behavior. *Journal of Labor Economics,* 24(3), 411-482.

Heppen, J.B., and Therriault, S.B. (2009). *Developing early warning systems to identify potential high school dropouts.* National High School Center. Available: http://www.betterhighschools. org/pubs/ews_guide.asp.

Hurst, D., Kelly, D., and Princiotta, D. (2004). *Educational attainment of high school dropouts 8 years later.* Washington, DC: U.S. Department of Education, National Center for Education Statistics. Available: http://nces.ed.gov/pubs2005/2005026.pdf.

Indiana Department of Education. (2008). *Dropout and mobility report.* Available: http://www.doe. in.gov/stn/pdf/2007-DM.pdf.

Ingels, S.J., Dowd, K.L., Taylor, J.R., Bartot, V.H., Frankel, M.R., Pulliam, P.A., and Quinn, P. (1995). *User's manual, NELS:88 second follow-up: Transcript component data file.* NCES 95377. Washington, DC: U.S. Department of Education, National Center for Education Statistics.

Jerald, C.D. (2006, June). *Identifying potential dropouts: Key lessons for building an early warning data system.* White paper prepared by Craig D. Jerald for Staying the Course: High Standards and Improved Graduation Rates, a joint project of Achieve, Inc., and Jobs for the Future. Washington, DC: Achieve, Inc.

Joftus, S. (2002). *Every child a graduate: A framework for an excellent education for all middle and high school students.* Washington, DC: Alliance for Excellent Education.

Jordan, W.J., Lara, J., and McPartland, J.M. (1999). Rethinking the cause of high school dropout. *Prevention Researcher, 6*, 1-4.

Kaufman, P. (2001). *The national dropout data collection system: Assessing consistency.* Paper prepared for the forum of the Civil Rights Project of Harvard University and Achieve, Inc., entitled Dropouts in America: How Severe Is the Problem? What Do We Know About Intervention and Prevention? Harvard University, January 13.

Kaufman, P. (2004). The national dropout data collection system: History and the search for consistency. In G. Orfield (Ed.), *Dropouts in America: Confronting the graduation rate crisis.* Pp. 107-130. Cambridge, MA: Harvard Educational Publishing Group.

Kaufman, P., McMillen, M., and Bradby, D. (1992). *Dropout rates in the United States: 1991.* NCES 92129. Washington, DC: U.S. Department of Education, National Center for Education Statistics.

Klem, A.M., and Connell, J.P. (2004). Relationships matter: Linking teacher support to student engagement and achievement. *Journal of School Health, 74*(7), 262-273.

Kominski, R. (1990). Estimating the national high school dropout rate. *Demography, 27,* 303-311.

Kurlaender, M., Reardon, S., and Jackson, J. (2008). *Middle school predictors of high school achievement in three California school districts.* Santa Barbara: California Dropout Research Project. Available: http://cdrp.ucsb.edu/dropouts/pubs_reports.htm.

Laird, J., Cataldi, E.F., KewalRamani, A., and Chapman, C. (2008). *Dropout and completion rates in the United States: 2006.* NCES 2008053. Washington, DC: U.S. Department of Education, National Center for Education Statistics. Available: http://nces.ed.gov/pubs2008/2008053. pdf.

Laurence, J. (2008, forthcoming). The military performance of GED holders. In J.J. Heckman and P. Fontaine (Eds.), *The GED and the problem of noncongitive skills in America.* Chicago: University of Chicago Press.

Lee, V.E., and Burkham, D.T. (2000). *Dropping out of high school: The role of school organization and structure.* Paper prepared for the forum of the Civil Rights Project of Harvard University and Achieve, Inc., entitled Dropouts in America: How Severe Is the Problem? What Do We Know About Intervention and Prevention? Harvard University, January 13.

Levin, H. (1988). Cost-effectiveness and educational policy. *Educational Evaluation and Policy Analysis, 10,* 51-69.

Levin, H., Belfield, C., Muennig, P., and Rouse, C. (2007). *The costs and benefits of an excellent education for all of America's children.* New York: Teachers College, Columbia University.

Levin, H.M. and Belfield, C.R. (2007). Educational interventions to raise high school graduation rates. In C.R. Belfield and H.M. Levin (Eds.), *The price we pay: Economic and social consequences of inadequate education* (pp.177-199). Washington, DC: Brookings Institution.

Linn, R. (2005). *Fixing the NCLB accountability system.* CRESST Policy Brief 8. Los Angeles: National Center for Research on Evaluation, Standards, and Student Testing.

Lleras-Muney, A. (2005). The relationship between education and adult mortality in the United States. *Review of Economic Studies, 721,* 189-221.

Lochner, L., and Moretti, E. (2004). The effect of education on crime: Evidence from prison, arrests, and self-reports. *American Economic Review, 94,* 155-189

Losen, D. (2008). *Graduation rates and federal policy: The changing landscape of reporting and accountability since 2001.* Paper prepared for the workshop of the Committee on Improved Measurement of High School Dropout and Completion Rates: Expert Guidance on Next Steps for Research and Policy, National Research Council, Washington, DC, October 23-24. Available: http://www7.nationalacademies.org/bota/High_School_Dropouts_Workshop_ Agenda.html.

Manlove, J. (1998). The influence of high school dropout and school disengagement on the risk of school-age pregnancy. *Journal of Research on Adolescence, 8*(2), 187-220.

Mare, R.D. (1980). Social background and school continuation decisions. *Journal of the American Statistical Association, 75,* 295-305.

McLanahan, S. (2009). Fragile families and the reproduction of poverty. *Annals of the American Academy of Political and Social Science, 621,* 111-131.

McPartland, J., and Jordan, W. (2001, January.). *Essential components of high school dropout prevention reforms.* Paper prepared for the forum of the Civil Rights Project of Harvard University and Achieve, Inc., entitled Dropouts in America: How Severe Is the Problem? What Do We Know About Intervention and Prevention? Harvard University, January 13.

Miao, J., and Haney, W. (2004, October 15). High school graduation rates: Alternative methods and implications. *Education Policy Analysis Archives, 12*(55). Available: http://epaa.asu.edu/ojs/article/viewFile/210/336.

Miller, S.R., and Gladden, R.M. (2002). *Changing special education enrollments: Causes and distribution among schools.* Paper presented at the Consortium on Chicago School Research. Available: http://ccsr.uchicago.edu/publications/p54.pdf.

Mishel, L. (2006). The exaggerated dropout crisis. *Education Week, 40.*

Mishel, L., and Roy, J. (2006). *Rethinking high school graduation rates and trends.* Washington, DC: Economic Policy Institute.

Moretti, E. (2007). Crime and the costs of criminal justice. In C.R. Belfield and H.M. Levin (Eds.), *The price we pay: Economic and social consequences of inadequate education* (pp.142-159.). Washington, DC: Brookings Institution.

Muennig, P. (2005, October). *Health returns to education interventions.* Paper prepared for the Equity Symposium on "The Social Costs of Inadequate Education," October 24-25, 2000, Teachers' College, Columbia University.

Murnane, R.J., Willett, J.B., and Boudett, K.P. (1995). Do high school dropouts benefit from obtaining a GED? *Educational Evaluation and Policy Analysis, 17*(2), 133-147.

Murnane, R.J., Willett, J.B., and Tyler, H.H. (2002, January). *Who benefits from obtaining a GED? Evidence from high school and beyond.* NASCALL Report. Available: http://www.ncsall.net/?id=771&pid=658.

National Center for Education Statistics. (1990). *A profile of the American eighth grader.* Washington, DC: U.S. Department of Education.

National Center for Education Statistics. (1992). *Characteristics of at-risk students in NELS:88.* Report No. 92–042. Washington, DC: U.S. Department of Education.

National Forum on Education Statistics. (2005). *Building a culture of data quality.* Available http://nces.ed.gov/forum/pub_2005801.asp [accessed September 23, 2009].

National Forum on Education Statistics. (2006). *Accounting for every student: A taxonomy of student exit codes.* Washington, DC: National Center for Education Statistics, U.S. Department of Education.

National Forum on Education Statistics. (2009, February). *Every school day counts.* Available http://nces.ed.gov/pubSearch/pubsinfo.asp?pubid=2009804 [accessed September 23, 2009].

National Governors Association Task Force on State High School Graduation Data. (2005). *Graduation counts.* Washington, DC: Author. Available: http://www.nga.org/Files/pdf/0507GRAD.PDF.

National Institute of Statistical Sciences and the Education Statistics Services Institute. (2005). *National Institute of Statistical Sciences/Education Statistics Services Institute Task Force on Graduation, Completion, and Dropout Indicators: Final report.* NCES 2005-105. Available: http://nces.ed.gov/pubs2005/2005105.pdf.

National Research Council. (2001). *Understanding dropouts: Statistics, strategies, and high stakes testing.* Committee on Educational Excellence and Testing Equity. A. Beatty, U. Neisser, W.T. Trent, and J.P. Heubert (Eds.). Washington, DC: National Academy Press.

National Research Council. (2002). *Scientific research in education.* Committee on Scientific Principles of Educational Research. R.J. Shavelson and L.S.Towne (Eds.). Washington, DC: National Academy Press.

National Research Council. (2004). *Keeping score for all: The effects of inclusion and accommodation policies on large-scale educational assessment.* Committee on Participation of English Language Learners and Students with Disabilities in NAEP and Other Large-Scale Assessments. J.A. Koenig and L.F. Bachman (Eds.). Washington, DC: The National Academies Press.

National Research Council. (2010). *Student mobility: Exploring the impacts of frequent moves on achievement.* Committee on the Impact of Mobility and Change on the Lives of Young Children, Schools, and Neighborhoods. A. Beatty (Ed.). Washington, DC: The National Academies Press.

National Research Council. (in press). *Allocating federal funds for state programs for English language learners.* Panel to Review Alternative Data Sources for the Limited-English Proficiency Allocation Formula under Title III, Part A, Elementary and Secondary Education Act. Committee on National Statistics and Board on Testing and Assessment. Division of Behavioral and Social Sciences and Education. Washington, DC: The National Academies Press.

Natriello, G., McDill, E.L., and Pallas, A.M. (1990). *Schooling disadvantaged children: Racing against catastrophe.* New York: Teachers College Press.

Neild, R., and Balfanz, R. (2006b). An extreme degree of difficulty: The educational demographics of urban neighborhood high schools. *Journal of Education for Students Placed at Risk, 11*(2), 123-141.

Nield, R.C., and Farley, E. (2004). Whatever happened to the class of 2000? The timing of dropouts in Philadelphia's schools. In G. Orfield (Ed.), *Dropouts in America.* Cambridge, MA: Harvard Educational Publishing Group.

Nield, R.C., Stoner-Eby, S., and Furstenburg, F.F. (2001, January). *Connecting entrance and departure: The transition to ninth grade and high school dropout.* Paper prepared for the forum of the Civil Rights Project of Harvard University and Achieve, Inc., entitled Dropouts in America: How Severe Is the Problem? What Do We Know About Intervention and Prevention? Harvard University, January 13.

Oreopoulos, P. (2007). Do dropouts drop out too soon? Wealth, health, and happiness from compulsory schooling. *Journal of Public Economics, 91,* 2213-2229.

Oreopoulos, P., and Salvanes, K.G. (2009). *How large are the returns to schooling? Hint: Money isn't everything.* NBER Working Paper No. 15339. Washington, DC: National Bureau of Economic Research. Available: http://papers.nber.org.proxy.library.ucsb.edu:2048/papers/w15339.

Orfield, G. (2004). *Dropouts in America: Confronting the graduation rate crisis.* Cambridge, MA: Harvard Educational Publishing Group.

Orfield, G., and Lee, C. (2006). *Racial transformation and the changing nature of segregation.* The Civil Rights Project. Cambridge, MA: Harvard University.

Pallas, A.M. (1989). *Making schools more responsive to at-risk students.* New York: ERIC Clearinghouse on Urban Education.

Pallas, A.M. (1990). Conceptual and measurement issues in the study of school dropouts. In R.G.C. and K. Namboodiri (Eds.), *Research in the sociology of education and socialization.* Greenwich, CT: JAI Press.

Pallas, A.M., Natriello, G., and McDill, E.L. (1989). The changing nature of the disadvantaged population: Current dimensions and future trends. *Educational Researcher, 18*(5), 16-22.

Parthenon Group. (2007). *Strategic planning to serve off-track youth: Data review and strategic implications.* Boston, MA: Parthenon Group. Available: http://8.12.35.242/files/Parthenon%20complete%20report.pdf.

Pleis, J.R., and Lucas, J.W. (2009). Summary health statistics for U.S. adults: National Health Interview Survey, 2007. *Vital and Health Statistics 10*(240), 1-159. Available: http://www.cdc.gov/nchs/data/series/sr_10/sr10_240.pdf.

Porter, A.C. (1991). Creating a system of school process indicators. *Educational Evaluation and Policy Analysis, 13,* 13-29.

Roderick, M., and Camburn, E. (1999). Risk and recovery from course failure in the early years of high school. *American Educational Research Journal, 36,* 303-343.

Roderick, M., Easton, J.Q., and Sebring, P.B. (2009). *The consortium on Chicago school research: A new model for the role of research in supporting urban school reform.* University of Chicago Urban Education Institute. Chicago: Consortium on Chicago School Research. Available: http://ccsr.uchicago.edu/content/publications.php?pub_id=131.

Ross, C.E., and Wu, C. (1995). The links between education and health. *American Sociological Review, 60*(5), 719-745.

Ross, C.E., and Wu, C. (1996). Education, age, and the cumulative advantage in health. *Journal of Health and Social Behavior, 37*(1), 104-120.

Rossi, R., and Montgomery, A. (1994). *Educational reforms and students at risk: A review of the current state of the art.* Washington, DC: American Institutes of Research.

Rothstein, R. (2008). *Why are indicators of dropout and completion rates important for policy and practice?* Paper prepared for the workshop of the Committee on Improved Measurement of High School Dropout and Completion Rates: Expert Guidance on Next Steps for Research and Policy, National Research Council, Washington, DC, October 23-24. Available: http://www7.nationalacademies.org/bota/High_School_Dropouts_Workshop_Agenda.html.

Rouse, C. (2005, October 24). *Labor market consequences of an inadequate education.* Paper prepared for the Symposium on the Social Costs of Inadequate Education, New York.

Rumberger, R.W. (1983). High school dropouts: A review of issues and evidence. *Review of Educational Research, 20,* 101-121.

Rumberger, R.W. (1987). High school dropouts: A review of issues and evidence. *Review of Educational Research, 57,* 101-121.

Rumberger, R.W. (1995). Dropping out of high school: The influence of race, sex, and family background. *American Educational Research Journal, 20*(2), 199-220.

Rumberger, R.W. (2008). *How longitudinal data systems can improve high school graduation rates.* Presentation prepared for the workshop of the Committee on Improved Measurement of High School Dropout and Completion Rates: Expert Guidance on Next Steps for Research and Policy, National Research Council, Washington, DC, October 23-24. Available: http://www7.nationalacademies.org/bota/High_School_Dropouts_Workshop_Agenda.html.

Rumberger, R.W. (2009). *What the federal government can do to improve high school performance.* Washington, DC: Center on Education Policy. Available: http://www.cep-dc.org/index.cfm?fuseaction=Page.viewPage&pageId=536&parentID=481.

Rumberger, R.W. (forthcoming). *Dropping out: Why students quit school and what can be done about it.* Cambridge, MA: Harvard University Press.

Rumberger, R.W., and Arellano, B. (2007). *Student and school predictors of high school graduation in California.* Santa Barbara: California Dropout Research Project, University of California.

Rumberger, R.W., and Lim, S.A. (2008). *Why students drop out of school: A review of 25 years of research.* Santa Barbara: California Dropout Research Project. Available: http://cdrp.ucsb.edu/dropouts/pubs_reports.htm.

Rumberger, R.W., and Palardy, G.J. (2005). Does segregation still matter? The impact of student composition on academic achievement in high school. *Teachers College Record, 107,* 1999-2045.

Rumberger, R.W., and Rotermund, S. (2008). *What happened to dropouts from the high school class of 2004?* Statistical Brief 10. Santa Barbara: California Dropout Research Project, University of California. Available: http://cdrp.ucsb.edu/dropouts/pubs_statbriefs.htm.

Schneider, B., Carnoy, M., Kilpatrick, J., Schmidt, W.H., and Shavelson, R.J. (2007). *Estimating causal effects using experimental and observational designs.* Report from the Governing Board of the American Educational Research Association Grants Program. Washington, DC: American Educational Research Association.

Seastrom, M., Hoffman, L., Chapman, C., and Stillwell, R. (2006a). *The average freshman graduation rate for public high schools from the Common Core of Data: School years 2002-03 and 2003-04.* NCES 2006-606rev. Washington, DC: U.S. Department of Education, National Center for Education Statistics.

Seastrom, M., Chapman, C., Stillwell, R., McGrath, D., Peltola, P., Dinkes, R., and Xu, Z. (2006b). *A review and analysis of alternative high school graduation rates, volume 1. Users guide to computing high school graduation rates, volume 2, an analysis of alternative high school graduation rates.* NCES 2006-604 and 605. Washington, DC: U.S. Department of Education, National Center for Education Statistics.

Sellers, J. (2007). *Florida's education pipeline: An overview.* Presentation made at the Conference on Finding the Right Port in a Storm: Strengthening the Connection Between Higher Education and State Workforce Development Goals, June 25-26. Denver: Western Interstate Commission for Higher Education. Available: http://www.wiche.edu/Policy/Ford/Forum0607/.

Shavelson, R., McDonnell, L., Oakes, J., and Carey, N. (1987). *Indicator systems for monitoring mathematics and science education.* Santa Monica, CA: RAND.

Silver, D., Saunders, M., and Zarate, E. (2008). *What factors predict high school graduation in the Los Angeles Unified School District?* Santa Barbara: California Dropout Research Project. Available http://cdrp.ucsb.edu/dropouts/pubs_reports.htm [accessed October 30, 2009].

Smith, B. (2008). *How can states build and maintain robust longitudinal data systems for collecting the requisite data to compute these indicators and to improve these outcomes?* Presentation prepared for the workshop of the Committee on Improved Measurement of High School Dropout and Completion Rates: Expert Guidance on Next Steps for Research and Policy, National Research Council, Washington, DC, October 23-24. Available: http://www7. nationalacademies.org/bota/High_School_Dropouts_Workshop_Agenda.html.

Snyder, T.D., Dillow, S.A., and Hoffman, C.M. (2008). *Digest of education statistics, 2007.* NCES #2008-022. Washington, DC: U.S. Government Printing Office.

Snyder, T.D., Dillow, S.A., and Hoffman, C.M. (2009). *Digest of education statistics, 2008.* NCES 2008-022. Washington, DC: U.S. Department of Education, National Center for Education Statistics. Available: http://nces.ed.gov/pubsearch/pubsinfo.asp?pubid=2009020.

Snyder, T.D., and Dillow, S.A. (2010). *Digest of education statistics 2009.* NCES 2010-013. Washington, DC: U.S. Government Printing Office. Available: http://nces.ed.gov/pubsearch/ pubsinfo.asp?pubid=2010013.

Supovitz, J.A. (2006). *The case for district-based reform: Leading, building, and sustaining school improvement.* Cambridge, MA: Harvard Education Publishing Group.

Swanson, C.B. (2003). *Keeping count and losing count: Calculating graduation rates for all students under NCLB accountability.* Washington, DC: Urban Institute. Available: http://www.urban. org/publications/410848.html.

Swanson, C.B. (2004). *The real truth about low graduation rates: An evidence-based commentary.* Washington, DC: Urban Institute. Available: http://www.urban.org/UploadedPDF/411050_ realtruth.pdf.

Swanson, C.B., and Chaplin, D. (2003). *Counting high school graduates when graduates count: Measuring graduation rates under the high stakes of NCLB.* Education Policy Center. Washington, DC: Urban Institute. Available: http://www.inpathways.net/nclb-grad.pdf.

Taylor, R. (2008). *Delaware: Dropouts, data, and discussion.* Presentation prepared for the workshop of the Committee on Improved Measurement of High School Dropout and Completion Rates: Expert Guidance on Next Steps for Research and Policy, National Research Council, Washington, DC, October 23-24. Available: http://www7.nationalacademies.org/bota/ High_School_Dropouts_Workshop_Agenda.html.

Thornburgh, N. (April, 2006). Dropout nation. *Time Magazine, 167*(16). Available: http://www. time.com/time/covers/0,16641,20060417,00.html

Thurgood, L., Walter, E., Carter, G., Henn, S., Huang, G., and Nooter, D. (2003). *NCES handbook of survey methods.* Washington, DC: U.S. Department of Education, National Center for Education Statistics. Available: http://nces.ed.gov/pubsearch/pubsinfo.asp?pubid=2003603.

Tyler, J.H. (2003). The economic benefits of the GED: Lessons from recent research. *Review of Educational Research, 73*(3), 369-403.

Tyler, J.H., Murnane, R.J., and Willett, J.B. (2000). Estimating the labor market signaling value of the GED. *Quarterly Journal of Economics,* 431-468.

Tyler, J.H., Murnane, R.J., and Willett, J.B. (2003). Who benefits from a GED? Evidence for females from high school and beyond. *Economics of Education Review 22*(3), 237-247.

U.S. Census Bureau. (2006). *Income, poverty, and health insurance coverage in the United States: 2005.* Washington, DC: U.S. Department of Commerce.

U.S. Department. of Education. (2008). *New race and ethnicity guidance for the collection of federal education data.* Available: http://www.ed.gov/policy/rschstat/guid/raceethnicity/indix.html. Modified 08/08/2008.

U.S. Department of Education. (2006). *Digest of education statistics, 2005.* Washington, DC: U.S. Department of Education, National Center for Education Statistics.

U.S. Department of Education. (2008a). *Digest of education statistics: Tables 382, 384, and 389.* Available: http://nces.ed.gov/programs/digest/2008menu_tables.asp.

U.S. Department of Education (2008b). *A uniform, comparable graduation rate: How the final regulations for Title I hold schools, districts, and states accountable for improving graduation rates.* Available: http://www2.ed.gov/policy/elsec/reg/proposal/uniform-grad-rate.html.

U.S. Department of Education. (2009). *American Recovery and Reinvestment Act of 2009: Using ARRA funds to drive school reform and improvement.* Washington, DC: Author.

U.S. Department of Education, Institute of Education Sciences, What Works Clearinghouse. (2008). *WWC topic report: Dropout prevention.* Available: http://ies.ed.gov/ncee/wwc/.

Uslaner, E.M., and Brown, M. (2005). Inequality, trust, and civic engagement. *American Politics Research, 33*(6), 868-894.

Warren, J.R. (2004). *State-level high school completion rates: Concepts, measures, and trends.* Paper presented at the annual meeting of the American Sociological Association, Atlanta.

Warren, J.R. (2005). State-level high school completion rates: Concepts, measures, and trends. *Education Policy Analysis Archives, 13.* Available: http://epaa.asu.edu/epaa/v13n51/.

Warren, J.R. (2008). *What are we trying to measure and how should we measure it? Conceptual and technical issues in the construction of high school dropout and completion rates.* Paper prepared for the workshop for the Committee on Improved Measurement of High School Dropout and Completion Rates: Expert Guidance on Next Steps for Research and Policy, National Research Council, Washington, DC, October 23-24. Available: http://www7.nationalacademies.org/bota/High_School_Dropouts_Workshop_Agenda.html.

Warren, J.R., and Halpern-Manners, A. (2007). Is the glass emptying or filling up? Reconciling divergent trends in high school completion and dropout. *Educational Researcher, 36*(6), 335-343.

Warren, J.R., and Halpern-Manners, A. (forthcoming). Measuring high school graduation rates at the state level: What difference does methodology make? *Sociological Methods and Research 38,* 3-37.

Western, B., and Wildeman, C. (2009). The black family and mass incarceration. *Annals of the American Academy of Political and Social Science, 621,* 221-242.

Whelage, G.G., and Rutter, R.A. (1986). Dropping out: How much do schools contribute to the problem? *Teachers College Record, 87,* 374-392.

Winglee, M., Marker, D., Hendersen, A., Young, B.A., and Hoffman, L. (2000). *A recommended approach to providing high school dropout and completion rates at the state level.* NCES 2000305. Washington, DC: U.S. Department of Education, National Center for Education Statistics.

Wong, M., Shapiro, M., Boscardin, W., and Ettner, S. (2002). Contribution of major diseases to disparities in mortality. *New England Journal of Medicine, 347*(20), 1585-1592.

Young, B., and Hoffman, L. (2002). *Public high school dropouts and completers from the common core of data: School years 1991-92 through 1997-98.* NCES 2002317. Washington, DC: U.S. Department of Education, National Center for Education Statistics.

A

Workshop Agenda and Participants

AGENDA

October 23, 2008

9:45 am   Welcome, Overview of the Workshop
           Robert Hauser, National Research Council, Washington, DC,
           and University of Wisconsin, Madison, *Chair*

**Why are indicators of dropout and completion rates important for policy
and practice?**
Moderator: Elaine Allensworth, Consortium on Chicago School Research
(committee member)

10:00   *Presentations*
           • Dan Losen, Civil Rights Project
           • Richard Rothstein, Economics Policy Institute
           • Delegate Ana Sol Gutiérrez, Maryland State Legislature

11:30   Break

11:45   *Discussants/Reactors*
               How are these rates used? What are the challenges associated
               with collecting the needed data?

               - Mel Riddile, National Association of Secondary School
                 Principals
               - Jeanine Hildreth, Baltimore City Schools
               - Noelle Ellerson, American Association of School
                 Administrators

12:15 pm   *Discussion with the Committee*
               Discussion Leader: Russell Rumberger, University of
               California, Santa Barbara (committee member)

               What are the key points the committee should consider in
               making recommendations about these rates?

12:45   Working lunch to continue discussion of key issues

Calculating the rates: What decisions are required, what data are required, what are the different ways of calculating the rates, and what are their strengths and weaknesses?
Moderator: Lavan Dukes, Florida Department of Education (committee member)

1:45   *Presentations*
               - Elaine Allensworth
               - J. Rob Warren, University of Minnesota (committee
                 member)

2:45   Break

3:00   *Discussants*
               Aaron Pallas, Teachers College, Columbia University
               Chris Swanson, Editorial Projects in Education

3:40   *Discussion with the Committee*
               Discussion Leader: Robert Hauser

               What are the key points the committee should consider in
               making recommendations about these rates?

4:30   Adjourn

October 24, 2008

8:30 am   Working continental breakfast to review goals of workshop

9:00   Welcome, Overview of the Day's Plan
                   Robert Hauser

How can states build and maintain robust longitudinal data systems for collecting the requisite data to compute these indicators and to improve these outcomes?
Moderator: Rob Warren

9:15   *Presentations*
- Nancy Smith, Data Quality Campaign
- Lavan Dukes
- Wesley Bruce, Indiana Department of Education
- Bill Smith, Sioux Falls School District, SD (by phone)
- Robert Curtin, Massachusetts Department of Education

11:00   Break

11:15   *Discussants*
                   Deborah Newby, U.S. Department of Education
                   Robin Taylor, Delaware Department of Education

11:45   *Discussion with the Committee*
                   Discussion Leader: Robert Hauser

                   What are the key points the committee should consider in making recommendations about these rates?

12:15 pm   Working lunch to continue discussion of key issues

How can the data from these systems be used to improve policy and practice?
Moderator: Lavan Dukes

1:15   *Presentations*
- Russell Rumberger
- Robert Balfanz, Johns Hopkins University

2:15   *Discussants*
                   David Wakelyn, National Governors Association
                   Ana Sol Gutiérrez, Maryland State Legislature

3:00	*Discussion with the Committee* Discussion Leader: Elaine Allensworth
	What are the key points the committee should consider in making recommendations about these rates?
3:30	Break
3:45	Synthesis of main messages Discussion Leader: Robert Hauser
4:30	Adjourn

PARTICIPANTS

Elaine Allensworth, Consortium on Chicago School Research
Alyssa Alston, Council of Chief State School Officers
Jason Amos, Alliance for Excellent Education
Robert Balfanz, Johns Hopkins University
James Bergeron, U.S. Congress, House Education, Labor, and Pensions
    Committee
Wesley Bruce, Indiana Department of Education
Mike Casserly, Council of Greater City Schools
Christopher Chapman, U.S. Department of Education
Robert Curtin, Massachusetts Department of Education
Elizabeth Demarest, SRI
G. Lavan Dukes, Florida Department of Education
Mark Dynarski, Mathematica
Noelle Ellerson, American Association of School Administrators
Stuart Elliott, National Research Council
Meredith Farace, U.S. Department of Education
Michael Feuer, National Research Council
Rebecca Fitch, U.S. Department of Education
Daria Hall, Education Trust
Andrew Halpern-Manners, University of Minnesota
Robert Hauser, National Research Council, and University of Wisconsin,
    Madison
Kati Haycock, Education Trust
Jeanine Hildreth, Baltimore City Schools
David Hoff, *Education Week*
Lee Hoffman, U.S. Department of Education
Judith Koenig, National Research Council
Dan Losen, Civil Rights Project, University of California, Los Angeles

Lawrence Mishel, Economics Policy Institute
Patricia Morison, National Research Council
Deborah Newby, U.S. Department of Education
Lynn Olsen, *Education Week*
Aaron Pallas, Teachers College, Columbia University
Lyndsay Pinkus, Alliance for Excellent Education
Mel Riddile, National Association of Secondary School Principals
Richard Rothstein, Economics Policy Institute
Russell Rumberger, University of California, Santa Barbara
Bill Smith, Sioux Falls School District, South Dakota (by phone)
Nancy Smith, Data Quality Campaign
Ana Sol Gutiérrez, Maryland State Legislature
Andrea Solarz, National Academy of Education
Chris Swanson, Editorial Projects in Education
Robin Taylor, Delaware Department of Education
David Wakelyn, National Governors Association
John Robert Warren, University of Minnesota
Gregory White, National Academy of Education

B

Biographical Sketches of
Committee Members and Staff

Robert M. Hauser (*Chair*) is executive director, Division of Behavioral and Social Sciences and Education at the National Research Council, and Vilas Research Professor, Emeritus, at the University of Wisconsin, Madison, where he has directed the Center for Demography and Ecology and the Institute for Research on Poverty. He has worked on the Wisconsin Longitudinal Study since 1969 and directed it since 1980. His current research interests include trends in educational progression and social mobility in the United States among racial and ethnic groups, the uses of educational assessment as a policy tool, the effects of families on social and economic inequality, changes in socioeconomic standing, health, and well-being across the life course. Hauser has contributed to studies of educational performance and attainment; he has directed a national study of social mobility; and his Wisconsin Longitudinal Study has followed the life course of 10,000 Wisconsin high school graduates and their families for almost 50 years. He has contributed to statistical methods for discrete multivariate analysis and structural equation models and to methods for the measurement of social and economic standing. He is a member of the National Academy of Sciences and the American Philosophical Society, and he is a fellow of the American Academy of Arts and Sciences, the American Statistical Association, and the American Association for the Advancement of Science. At the National Research Council (NRC), he has served on the Committee on National Statistics, the Division of Behavioral and Social Sciences and Education, and the Board on Testing and Assessment. He has also served on numerous NRC research panels and chaired panel studies of high-stakes testing and standards for adult literacy. He recently served on the secretary of education's task force on the measurement of high school dropout rates. He has a B.A. in economics from the University of Chicago and M.A. and Ph.D. degrees in sociology from the University of Michigan.

Elaine Allensworth is the interim coexecutive director of the Consortium on Chicago School Research at the University of Chicago. She conducts research on the structural factors that affect high school students' educational attainment, particularly the factors that affect graduation and dropout rates. Her body of work includes research on school organizational structure, instruction, and early indicators of dropping out. Her research is funded by the Bill and Melinda Gates Foundation, the Carnegie Corporation of New York, the National Science Foundation, and the Institute of Education Sciences at the U.S. Department of Education. Currently she is leading a mixed-methods study of the transition to high school, as well as studies on the effects of curricular reforms on instruction, grades, test scores, high school graduation, and college attendance. She has a Ph.D. in sociology and an M.A. in urban studies from Michigan State University and was once a high school teacher.

G. Lavan Dukes is the educational policy development director at the Florida Department of Education. In this role, he establishes policy direction for the database of information on students and teachers in the Florida state public school system. He also provides policy guidance to staff regarding the department's major statistical publications and presentations and serves as representative of the state commissioner on issues dealing with state and federal reporting requirements. He led the work to establish student and staff databases that are the basis of Florida's Education Data Warehouse. He has served on many national task forces and committees dealing with data reporting, systems design, and student, staff, and financial information systems. He currently serves as Florida's representative on the National Cooperative Education Statistics System and on the Education Information Management Advisory Committee of the Council of Chief State School Officers. At the National Research Council, he served on the Committee on Improving Measures of Access to Equal Educational Opportunity. His career began as a middle school English teacher. He has an M.A. in education from Florida State University.

Kenji Hakuta is the Lee J. Jacks Professor of Education at Stanford University. An experimental psycholinguist by training, he is best known for his work in the areas of bilingualism and the acquisition of English by immigrant students. Hakuta is also active in education policy. He has testified before Congress and other public bodies on language policy, the education of language-minority students, affirmative action in higher education, and improving the quality of education research. He has served as an expert witness in education litigation involving language-minority students. He has been on the faculty at Stanford since 1989, except for three years (2003-2006) when he helped start the University of California at Merced as its founding dean of social sciences, humanities, and arts. He was a fellow at the Center for Advanced Study in the Behavioral Sciences, is an elected member of the National Academy of Education, and is a fellow of the American Association for the Advancement of Science (Linguistics and Language Sciences). He currently serves on the board of the Educational Testing Service and as vice-chair of the board of the Spencer Foundation. At the National Research Council, Hakuta chaired the Committee on Developing a Research Agenda on the Education of Limited English Proficient and Bilingual Students and served on the Committee on Educational Excellence and Testing Equity. He has a B.A. (magna cum laude) in psychology and social relations and a Ph.D. in experimental psychology, both from Harvard University.

Judith A. Koenig (*Study Director*) is a senior program officer for the Board on Testing and Assessment. Since 1999, she has directed measurement-related studies designed to inform education policy, including studies of the National Assessment of Educational Progress and of assessments for teacher licensure and advanced-level certification, inclusion of special needs students in assessment programs, developing assessments for state and federal accountability programs, and setting standards for the National Assessment of Adult Literacy. From 1984 to 1999, she worked at the Association of American Medical Colleges on the Medical College Admission Test, directing operational programs and leading a comprehensive research program on the examination. Prior to that, she worked for 10 years as a special education teacher and diagnostician. She has a B.A. (1975) in special education from Michigan State University, an M.A. (1984) in psychology from George Mason University, and a Ph.D. (2003) in educational measurement, statistics, and evaluation from the University of Maryland.

Russell W. Rumberger is professor of education in the Gevirtz Graduate School of Education at the University of California (UC), Santa Barbara, and former director of the Linguistic Minority Research Institute, a UC multicampus research unit established in 1984 to foster interdisciplinary research and to improve academic achievement of children from diverse language backgrounds. A faculty member at Santa Barbara since 1987, he has published widely in the areas of education and work, the schooling of disadvantaged students, school effectiveness, and education policy. He has been conducting research on school dropouts for the past 25 years and has written numerous research papers and essays on the topic. He served as a member of the Task Force on Graduation, Completion, and Dropout Indicators of the U.S. Department of Education in 2004. At the National Research Council, he was a member of the Committee on Increasing High School Students' Engagement and Motivation to Learn and currently serves on the Committee on the Impact of Mobility and Change on the Lives of Young

Children, Schools, and Neighborhoods. He is currently directing the California Dropout Research Project. He has a B.S. in electrical engineering from Carnegie Mellon University and a Ph.D. in education and an M.A. in economics from Stanford University.

John Robert Warren is professor of sociology at the University of Minnesota. His research interests are inequalities in educational and health outcomes. His recent work focuses on the measurement of state high school completion rates, the consequences of state high school exit examinations for educational and labor market outcomes, the magnitude of "panel conditioning" (or time in survey) effects in longitudinal surveys, changes over time in the association between socioeconomic status and health, and the effects of life-course trajectories of work and family roles on health and financial outcomes in late adulthood. He has published numerous journal articles on these topics and recently served as deputy editor of the journal *Sociology of Education*. He has a B.A. in sociology and anthropology from Carleton College and M.S. and Ph.D. degrees in sociology from the University of Wisconsin, Madison.

Patricia I. Wright is the superintendent of public instruction in the Virginia Department of Education. She has served as deputy superintendent, assistant superintendent for instruction, director of secondary instruction, and state mathematics specialist in the Virginia Department of Education. During her more than 25 years with the Virginia Department of Education and 34 total years in public education, she has worked closely with the Board of Education, governors, the General Assembly, local school systems, and professional organizations to develop and implement Virginia's Standards of Learning accountability program, a graduation and completion index, and a statewide system of support for public schools. She currently serves as a member of the Council of Chief State School Officers ESEA (Elementary and Secondary Education Act) Reauthorization Task Force, a commissioner on the Education Commission of the States, and a member of the National High School Center Advisory Board. She also serves as a board member on the National Council for Accreditation of Teacher Education State Partnership, the Virginia Association of Secondary School Principals, and the Virginia Advanced Studies Strategies (National Mathematics and Science Initiative). She has a Ph.D. in mathematics education from the University of Virginia, an M.A. in mathematics education from Virginia Commonwealth University, and a B.A. in mathematics from James Madison University.